The VIDAL LECTURE

Sex and Politics in
Massachusetts, and the
Persecution of Chief Justice
Robert Bonin

James A. Aloisi, Jr.

Ashburton Hill
an imprint of Chilmark Books
Boston, Massachusetts USA
www.chilmark.co
+1 617-360-8200

For ordering information and for
permission to reproduce selections
from this book, please write to:

ashburtonhill@chilmark.co

ISBN-13: 978-0-97882591-1

Book and Cover Design by Eric Mulder
Set in Garamond

Printed in the United States of America

For Alec Gray

1952-2005

When to the sessions of sweet silent thought
I summon up remembrance of things past,
I sigh the lack of many a thing I sought,
And with old woes new wail my dear time's waste;

But if the while I think on thee, dear friend,
All losses are restor'd, and sorrows end.

Sonnet #30, William Shakespeare

"I am a man more sinn'd against than sinning."

❧

King Lear, Act III, Scene 2.

"For nothing is lost, nothing is ever lost.   There is always the clue, the canceled check, the smear of lipstick, the footprint in the canna bed . . . And all times are one time, and all those dead in the past never lived before our definition gives them life, and out of the shadow their eyes implore us."

❧

All the King's Men, Robert Penn Warren

Revere Beach

*T*HE BEACH HAD *always been a place of refuge, first for immigrant city dwellers seeking light, air and recreation, and then later, in the early years of the twentieth century, for thrill seekers drawn to a magnificent state-of-the-art amusement park, and finally, when the families had gone and the amusements closed, for the lonely and the dispossessed, especially for certain men who sought out sex for hire among the boys who lingered along the boulevard.*

Revere Beach was once the gem of Boston's North Shore, a place memorialized in the late nineteenth century by a series of beautiful watercolors by Maurice Prendergast. But time and neglect eventually took their toll. By 1977, the beach had become a run down, depressing oceanfront strip, catering to a ragged and rough crowd seeking pleasure from a variety of illicit activities. The district attorney of Suffolk County decided to shut down the beach's reputation as a "boy town" by sending a powerful message through his indictment of twenty-four men for having sex with adolescent males. The district attorney was Garrett Byrne, a fixture in Boston politics, who was seeking re-election in 1978 at the age of eighty. Byrne was a powerful figure, not accustomed to being opposed in his crime fighting efforts, but on this occasion he was challenged by a fringe group of radical activists who chose to make the prosecutions of the so-called "Revere 24" a defining moment in their culture war against the establishment. Organized as the Boston/Boise Committee, these activists opposed what they viewed as a witch-hunt, and they would do so in a variety of ways, including fund raising for the defense of the men under indictment. Their most prominent fundraiser was held on an early April evening in 1978, in Boston's historic Arlington Street Church, where the internationally-acclaimed author and social critic, Gore Vidal, was invited to speak. Vidal's predictably provocative topic was "Sex and Politics in Massachusetts."

AN EVENING WITH GORE VIDAL

T HE FIFTY-ONE-YEAR-OLD author strikes a dashing figure as he rises to speak, and the restless audience is suddenly quiet because Gore Vidal is famous for being an engaging and provocative speaker. Vidal is witty at times, and outrageous, but most of what he has to say is rambling and disconnected, because on this night Vidal has no prepared text, and confesses that he is going to "wing it."[1]

Vidal inserts himself into the local scandal, arguing that the state's statutory rape and age of consent laws were out of synch with the times. "When you think of it," he says, "should there be such a thing as statutory rape? That sounds to me like a contradiction." Vidal observes that of the one hundred men serving life or multiple life sentences in Massachusetts for non-violent sex acts with boys under sixteen, "No force was used. The boys involved ... were not damaged and perfectly willing to go through this."[2]

Many of those assembled in the church understand exactly what Vidal is getting at. A large cadre of radical activists are present this evening, young men determined to challenge commonly accepted norms regarding intergenerational sex. Vidal's words give these activists comfort that they are not alone in their views. But there are others in the audience who do not share those views, citizens who have come with only one purpose: to hear a lecture given by a famous author. These audience members are not prepared to participate in a political rally and fundraiser.

The chief justice of the state's Superior Court, Robert Bonin, is in the audience. A week earlier, Bonin had seen the Vidal lecture advertised in the *Boston Globe,* and asked his wife Angela if she wanted to attend. She agreed, and they invited Professor Thomas Lambert and his wife to join them for what they thought was going to be a relaxing evening of drinks, dinner and conversation, followed by an interesting lecture by Vidal. Instead they find themselves in the middle of a long evening of speeches by people they do not know, for a cause they do not understand. Angela Bonin will recall the event as "a very discombobulated meeting."[3] Professor Lambert will later testify that the speeches that evening "were to be endured and not to be enjoyed ... the atmosphere was one of confusion."[4]

At the post-lecture reception, Bonin meets Vidal and playfully reproaches the author for some unkind Vidal-isms about the judiciary: "It's wrong to assume judges are troglodytes," Bonin tells the author.[5] Many years later Vidal would recall Bonin as "an amiable scholarly figure" who, following their light banter, asked the author to autograph his copy of *Burr*.[6] As the two men speak, someone takes their picture. That photograph, and another of Bob and Angela Bonin seated in the church, find their way to the newsroom of the *Boston Herald American,* and to the paper's front page the next day. In eight days, Bob Bonin's public career would effectively be over. Precisely what the chief justice knew about the event, and when he knew it, would become central elements of the final effort to remove him from office.

I N THE 1970s, there were two Bostons. One Boston was a staid, stagnant, lackluster place, a once proud city that had been left behind by the energy and modernity of larger, more exciting and sophisticated urban centers like New York, San Francisco and Los Angeles. But there was also the emerging "New Boston," an exciting metropolis symbolized by the new

Government Center and Prudential Center developments and the redevelopment of Faneuil Hall Marketplace. The New Boston was led by a young and energetic mayor, Kevin White, who himself was emblematic of a new generation of political leaders focused on reform and change—ambitious and talented men who were unwilling to wait their turn while the old guard remained stubbornly in office.

Massachusetts in 1978 was awash in the turbulence and discord that mark times of significant transition. A great political tug-of-war was taking place, a struggle between reformers and the established political leadership, and a larger struggle between two generations of political leaders. In 1978 three leading political figures—the incumbent governor, the incumbent United States senator, and the incumbent district attorney of Suffolk County—lost their respective bids for re-election, and the president of the Massachusetts Senate resigned amid a brewing scandal. In the midst of this turmoil Robert Bonin, the chief justice of the Commonwealth's Superior Court, was faced with a Hobson's choice: resignation or removal from office.

Beginning with Bonin's appointment as chief justice in 1977, a determined, entrenched legal and political establishment embarked upon an unrelenting effort to remove him from office. Their ultimately successful effort was one important victory in a war between cultures and generations—a clash of aging political leaders holding on to power with an iron grip, and young reformers reaching for power and, having grasped it, unwilling to let it go without a fight.

The political and cultural forces that converged to create such a tumultuous political moment were complex and deep-rooted, and they illuminated much about what Boston had been, and what it would become.

PART ONE

◇

Michael Dukakis and the
Struggle for Court Reform

CHAPTER 1

A Lawyer of Considerable Ability

MASSACHUSETTS WAS the only state in the nation that resisted the tidal wave of Richard Nixon's 1972 landslide. The Bay State's singular embrace of South Dakota Senator George McGovern cemented in the minds of many Americans the impression of Massachusetts as a bastion of liberal Democratic politics. That impression belied a more complicated truth. While city politics was reliably Democratic in the hands of the Irish politicians who dominated Boston through most of the twentieth century, Massachusetts was a two-party state, more often than not led by Republican governors. The sole exception to that general rule came during a brief snapshot in time, the twenty-year period between 1970 and 1990.

During those twenty years, Massachusetts was nearly completely dominated by the Democratic Party, and the Democratic Party was dominated by the legend and legacy of the Kennedy family. The ascent of John F. Kennedy, grandson of Boston mayor and ward boss John Francis "Honey Fitz" Fitzgerald, to the Congress and then to the presidency was remarkable in many respects. Kennedy's political career was a bridge between the insular ethnic politics of his grandfather's days and the reform minded impulses of the second half of the century.

The difference between the Massachusetts of the "Honey Fitz" era and the Massachusetts of the Kennedy era can be measured by more than the passage of time. For the larger part of the first half of the century Boston was dominated by men who were deeply connected to their European roots. But in the decades following midcentury those who entered politics did not look back to Europe for their identity. Special bonds connected these young men of the 1950s and 1960s to the idea of America as a place where everything was possible, a melting pot where old barriers began to fade. They were Americans first, and only secondarily sons of Ireland or Italy or wherever. They heard a different call, these men who, as John Kennedy memorably noted in his inaugural address, were "born in this century, tempered by war, disciplined by a hard and bitter peace, proud of [their] ancient heritage."[7]

In the 1960s, the landscape of Massachusetts politics was populated by two generations of ambitious men: the older generation who had known political power, had fought for it and forged lasting relationships doing so, and who were reluctant to give it up, and the newer generation epitomized by JFK but expressed at the local level by men with non-Irish ethnic names, names like Dukakis, Brooke and Bellotti. The new generation of leaders shared one thing with their old guard predecessors: the ambition for political power burned as brightly in them as it did in the ward bosses and mayors of the early twentieth century.

Among these new political leaders was a young criminal defense attorney from Quincy, Francis Xavier Bellotti. Born in Boston, Bellotti was a self-made man who had worked his way through college (Tufts) and law school (Boston College). A workaholic who rose each day at four, sported a military style crew cut and nursed a strong and seeming unquenchable ambition, Bellotti ran for Norfolk County district attorney in 1958 as a way to advertise his legal business. "I knew there was no way I was going to win," Bellotti recalled many years later, "[but] I decided to put up signs saying 'Attorney Francis X. Bellotti for District Attorney.' By the time the campaign was

Figure 1: "Politics Was His Lifestyle"
Frank Bellotti: A strict self-disciplinarian who would not accept defeat.

over, another few thousand people would know there was this lawyer around."[8] Bellotti proved adept at politics ("Once I got into it, I got all excited," he remembered), and while he lost that first election by 40,000 votes, he quickly emerged from obscurity as a formidable vote getter and force to be reckoned with.[9] As Massachusetts House Speaker Charles Flaherty put it, "Once Frank has someone, he's got them for life. That is just the sort of guy he is."[10]

Politics was more than Frank Bellotti's avocation. It was his lifestyle. He stood for state constitutional office in every election from 1962 through 1982, and again in 1990.[11] In 1962 he was the boy wonder of the Democratic Party, the fresh face who came out of nowhere to challenge the party regulars and win election as lieutenant governor against car salesman Herbert Connolly, beating Connolly in every county and amassing a one-hundred-thousand-vote margin. It was a political humiliation that Connolly—and the party regulars— would not easily forget.

Bellotti was a complicated man, a political loner who would shun obligatory events like the annual South Boston St. Patrick's Day breakfast, who spent more time working out at the YMCA than he did working the State House halls, whose obsession with fitness was offset by a fondness for red wine and Italian food, a father of twelve children who was frequently absent as he traveled the state looking for votes. He was masterful working a crowd, remembering names and dates and the place where he first met so-and-so and "how is your daughter doing, and wouldn't she be twelve years old now?" Bellotti immediately established a rapport, a sense of intimacy, with a person he barely knew or had not seen in years, with his "riveting eyes and a two-handed handshake that just bowled people over."[12]

Bellotti was a strict self-disciplinarian, a man who would not accept defeat or admit failure. "I have always assumed the other guys were smarter," he once said, "so I've always tried to outwork them."[13] He never let a challenge go unmet, and rarely forgot a slight. It showed in his political tenacity. It also showed in his uncompromising adherence to a physical fitness regimen. He would devote several hours each day to a rigorous training regimen, running, playing handball, swimming. When he was in the Navy, he once recalled, he was initially terrible at diving, and "there was a guy … [who] used to sit by the pool with his friends and drink martinis and they'd watch me and laugh when I took the dives. And at first I used to land on my stomach and scrape my nose on the bottom of the pool and they'd laugh. But when I finished I knew how to do fourteen different dives, all well. And they were still sitting there with their martinis, stiff."[14]

Even his detractors regarded Bellotti as a "lawyer of considerable ability," but "FXB" (as he was called) was never satisfied with the mere practice of law.[15] He had the same single-minded attraction to public service and politics that animated a more famous American lawyer/politician, Richard Nixon, whose career at a prestigious New York law firm in the years following his defeat to John Kennedy left him so unfulfilled that (as he recalled in his memoir) he was certain that if all he had was his legal work, he "would be mentally dead in two years and physically dead in four."[16] Like Nixon, Bellotti began his career with a bang, and then faced a long period of political exile, only to return triumphant.

Bellotti was also among those men, notably including State Secretary Kevin White and Attorney General Edward McCormack, who were determined to free themselves from the political dominance of the Kennedy family in Massachusetts politics. In the early 1960s, that dominance was at its zenith. In 1962 the bruising battle for John Kennedy's Senate seat between McCormack and the President's youngest brother,

Figure 2: "These Were Times When This Year's Ally Was Next Year's
Enemy"
Michael Dukakis keeps hands safely behind his back as Boston Mayor
Kevin White and Senator Edward Kennedy share a guarded handshake.

Edward, became a metaphor for the collision that was taking place between "regular" Massachusetts Democrats and the Kennedy Democrats.

Governor Endicott Peabody was a Kennedy Democrat riding the wave of Kennedy popularity in 1962 with a surprise (albeit slim) victory over incumbent Governor John Volpe. Through a strong relationship with Congressman Thomas P. "Tip" O'Neill, Peabody larded state government with O'Neill and Kennedy men. Young politicians like Bellotti and White were left with the dregs or with nothing at all to sustain their political organizations and build their futures. Edward Kennedy's decision to run for his older brother's Senate seat created more than a clash with the incumbent attorney general, Edward McCormack. It was a clear signal to every other office holder that they were expected to place their ambitions second to those of the Kennedy family.

Kevin White, for one, had not forgotten John Kennedy's unintended put down at the legendary Boston Garden rally that closed the 1960 campaign. Introducing the state's candidates for constitutional office that year, JFK referred to White—a man with strong roots in Boston politics—as "Calvin Witt."[17] White was elected State Secretary that year, and two years later he supported McCormack in the primary fight against Ted Kennedy. Now, as the 1964 election approached, White called for a meeting with Bellotti and McCormack. The three men, each determined to set his own fate, agreed to be supportive of one other in their respective future statewide races.[18]

Bellotti chose the boldest, riskiest course: the lieutenant governor would run against Peabody for governor in the Democratic primary. It was an unprecedented display of political ambition, but Bellotti backed up his challenge with a capacity for fundraising and hard work that was the envy of his peers. From Bellotti's perspective, he had been treated with disrespect as lieutenant governor, and would soon be eclipsed by others if he did not make a bold move. Years later Bellotti recalled the difficulties of serving as Peabody's lieutenant governor. "We'd go places and they would let Peabody speak but they wouldn't let me speak. I went to increase my budget and they really started screwing me around. In May I said 'I've had enough of this. I'm going to run.'"[19] Bellotti saw no choice but to make the run for governor. But he broke a cardinal rule in politics: he didn't wait his turn.[20]

At one point Bellotti was summoned to a meeting at Stephen Smith's apartment in New York City with Edward Kennedy, who asked him to refrain from running against Peabody. "Don't do this. Next time we will all be with you, Frank," Bellotti recalled Kennedy saying. But Bellotti was having none if it. He was convinced there would be no "next time," that rumors about Bobby Kennedy returning to Massachusetts to run for office someday might prove accurate, and where would he be then? He told Kennedy, "They threw me around for a year and a half. If Bobby decides to come back [to run in Massachusetts], you guys will kill me." Bellotti told Kennedy he would not quit, and Kennedy said "Things will never be the same with us, Frank." The die had been cast.[21]

Bellotti's race against Peabody in 1964 was considered "outrageous even by Massachusetts' standards."[22] It was a bruising primary battle, distinguished for its ethnic slurs and "uncivil personal attack[s]," and won decisively by Bellotti.[23] The victory was a costly one, leaving deep, lasting scars. During the general election campaign against former governor John Volpe, the electorate was filled with a steady diet of false rumors about Bellotti's ties to organized crime, and campaign advertisements asking whether the voters could, as did the defeated Governor Peabody, "trust" Bellotti?[24] Many did, but more didn't, and Bellotti lost one of the closest elections for governor in Massachusetts history.[25]

Bellotti did not know it, but he was about to enter a long period in the political wilderness. It would be ten years before he would win another race.

CHAPTER 2

The Reformers Take Charge

A S THE STATE'S POLITICAL titans battled each other in 1964, little attention was being paid to a young man who had taken office in 1963 as a state legislator representing his hometown of Brookline. Michael Dukakis was a full decade younger than Frank Bellotti, but their political careers in Massachusetts would overlap as they vied for the state's top political prize over the next three decades.

Dukakis began his political career as a liberal reformer. Unlike many of his contemporaries, he did not enter politics because it was in his family tradition, or because of an abiding need to exercise political power. For Dukakis, politics meant the ability to change things, to clean up a corrupt and lazy state government and reform inefficient systems.

In 1965, the Massachusetts Crime Commission had expressed its concern and outrage over widespread corruption in state government—corruption that went beyond the merely predictable world of bribery to include a patronage system unmoored from even the most rudimentary pretense of quality — "the spoils system allocation of jobs to political henchmen . . . [and] the now deeply ingrained view of government jobs and government business as a private preserve for taking care of those with political connections."[26] United States Senator Edward Brooke, writing of these times years later, recalled that a primary reason for his decision to enter politics was his "growing distaste for the political corruption" in Massachusetts. "Dishonesty was practiced not just by the corrupt at heart; good people were led into bribery and pay-offs, told this was the right way to proceed. It was a shameful mess."[27] That was the world Michael Dukakis meant to change.

Dukakis was young and in a hurry. "The Duke," as he was called, quickly made his mark in the Commonwealth's Legislature as the champion of "no fault" automobile insurance. He was "a persuasive debater . . . not loved by most of his colleagues, but widely respected."[28] Facing the wrath of the trial lawyers, who thrived on the complicated and contentious thicket of blame that grew out of existing practices, Dukakis worked with a dogged determination to implement an auto insurance reform program that served as a

Figure 3: "The Changing Face of Massachusetts Politics"
Michael Dukakis brought a determined focus to reforming "business as usual"
at the State House during his 12 years as governor.

national model. Despite this success, Dukakis understood that continued service in the Legislature did not offer him the best opportunity to fulfill his reform instincts. The independence that would come from achieving higher office appealed to him, and he moved quickly to position himself for a statewide race.

In 1966 Dukakis made a brief and unsuccessful effort to win his party's nomination for attorney general. He was defeated at the state convention by Bellotti, but the two men harbored no animosity against one another. Dukakis in defeat "handled himself with real class," Bellotti remarked at the time.[29] Four years later, Dukakis ran as the Democratic Party's nominee for lieutenant governor on a ticket led by Boston Mayor Kevin White. The White/Dukakis combination lost, but Dukakis used the race as an opportunity to boost his name recognition and build a statewide network of supporters. Smart, articulate and telegenic, Dukakis gained significant statewide exposure by hosting the popular public television program, *The Advocates*. Dukakis was well positioned to make his own successful run for governor in 1974. His campaign slogan declared immodestly that "Mike Dukakis should be Governor."[30]

Dukakis was an energetic campaigner with a talent for organizing at the grassroots. He understood that Massachusetts was moving in a different, more progressive direction and took full advantage of that understanding. He easily dispatched the incumbent attorney general, Robert Quinn, in the Democratic primary, and made quick work of the popular Republican incumbent governor, Francis Sargent, in the general election. Sargent famously declared that he lost the election because of the "price of hamburger," but it wasn't that simple. He had been beaten by one of the state's most skillful politicians.[31]

As Dukakis was winning an easy election victory in 1974, the Democratic candidate for attorney general, Frank Bellotti, found himself suffering through a long nail-biter of an evening. Bellotti had recovered from his 1964 loss to John Volpe and won his party's nomination for attorney general in 1966, but he was trounced in the general election by Republican Elliot Richardson after one of the dirtiest campaigns in Massachusetts history.

Richardson's campaign was buoyed by rumors of Bellotti's purported organized crime connections, rumors the Richardson camp nourished through an effective whispering campaign.[32] In an eleventh-hour ploy, Richardson accused Bellotti of having improperly received compensation from an Ohio insurance company while he was lieutenant governor.

Bellotti, said Richardson, lacked "moral sensitivity." He called on the state's attorney general, Edward Brooke, to conduct a grand jury investigation. It did not matter that the charges were untrue, or that Richardson offered no evidence to support his claims.[33] Coming as it did at the close of the campaign, Bellotti had no opportunity to effectively challenge the charges against him. He was tainted, and the stain was difficult to remove. (He would later be exonerated by a special commission established to review Richardson's charges).[34] In 1970, Bellotti ran again for governor, and placed third in a four-way primary. It seemed his political career was over, but Bellotti had one more race left in him.

1974 was a Democratic year. The post-Watergate feelings of animus toward the GOP were still fresh in the public memory and a stiff recession made most Republican candidates vulnerable to attack. Bellotti eagerly jumped into a crowded primary race for attorney general, where his years of campaigning and high name recognition would provide him with an important advantage. He also wanted to get lost in the political crowd. Bellotti believed that the distraction of the Watergate scandal helped him maintain his early advantage in a crowded field of unknowns. He recalled praying before the primary: "I hope

Nixon doesn't resign. Jesus, please Nixon, don't resign, nobody knows I'm running."[35]

Bellotti won the Democratic primary handily, and he was once again in a general election for statewide office. His opponent, the Yankee Republican Josiah Spaulding, could not resist raising the many ghosts and rumors that had plagued Bellotti since 1964. Spaulding spent much time during the campaign raising concerns about Bellotti's fitness to hold office, asking: "I don't know why Bellotti wants to be attorney general. Do you know?"[36] Michael Kenney, writing in the *Boston Globe*, pointed out that the "gut issue is Frank Bellotti: is he a decent man with serious concerns about personal liberty who can be vindicated after all these years and allowed to hold political office in Massachusetts, or is he still the evil force that Elliot Richardson conjured up?"[37] The *Boston Globe* was particularly brutal to Bellotti. The newspaper ran derogatory cartoons, endorsed Spaulding, and on the weekend before the general election ran a poll crediting Spaulding with a six percent lead over Bellotti.[38]

Haunted by the past, Bellotti called upon all of the resources at his disposal and made a deliberate effort to change his image. "They had banged me around so badly that I couldn't let them win," Bellotti would recall.[39] He was now wearing his hair long, sporting stylish clothes, and his campaign brochures referred to him as "Francis Bellotti." The point was clear: Bellotti meant to win, and he was shedding as many vestiges of his past to do so. What he did not know was: *would it be enough?*

Now, in the dark hours of a cold November evening, with Dukakis and the rest of the Democratic ticket having claimed early victories, Bellotti watched as his early lead slowly eroded. He worked the phones alone, from eleven-thirty that night until six the next morning, calling upon contacts throughout the state for information, leads, hope. Bellotti was a veteran of the election night ritual, and by four in the morning he thought he had the election won. When his wife Maggie woke a half-hour later and asked him "Was it worth it?" Bellotti had no answer. As he later explained, "When I knew I had finally won, there was no joy. No joy … I had won and that was what I had wanted to do and I didn't care anymore."[40]

The closeness of the final tally—less than twenty thousand votes out of nearly 1.9 million cast—made victory bittersweet. He had suffered defeats in three consecutive statewide elections, had seen his reputation tarnished and integrity questioned by

Republican opponents in 1964 and 1966, and had worked mightily to return to office and to prove himself as a man of honesty and ability. This victory was vindication, to be sure. On election night, Bellotti thanked his supporters, "so many people [who] have been helping me to crawl up the hill for ten years."[41] He would later recall: "They used to laugh at me when I tried to come back. But I did and I won."[42] When he emerged as the newly elected attorney general, Bellotti quickly sought to restore—or more accurately rebuild—his public image.

Bellotti in these years was described by one of his closest associates as a "man on a mission" who needed to "prove the world wrong about their impressions of him."[43] The reality was that Bellotti had always been a political maverick, not one of party regulars, but that was certainly not the impression he—or the media—left with the voters. The new attorney general therefore devoted considerable time demonstrating that he was an independent and a progressive leader.[44] On the day he was sworn in as attorney general, Bellotti went out of his way to ensure the public that his political ambition "has as its limits to make the Department of the Attorney General the best and most responsive to the needs of the people in the history of the nation."[45]

Much was symbolic, including his decision to move the entire attorney general's office out of the State House and into a new state office building across the street. Bellotti's selection of a man who had not even voted for him for the sensitive and influential post of "First Assistant Attorney General" was symbolic as well—a signal that this attorney general was going to break the mold.

In a political world dominated by patronage and personal loyalty, the very idea of offering the top appointment in the attorney general's office to anyone but a trusted associate, much less to someone who supported your campaign opponent, was unthinkable. It was certainly unprecedented. Bellotti understood that such an appointment would contribute in a large way to the image of a fresh, unconventional and apolitical law enforcement office that he was trying to build.

"I was a good trial lawyer," recalled Bellotti, "and I ran my own law office, but no one would know that—they all thought I was a hack. So I figured that I would make everybody work full time, and give up my law practice, and pick the best people I could find. And I went in there and found out who the good people were, kept them on, and then cleaned the place out. I figured that you can get loyalty by getting respect, even if you don't know the people."[46]

When he announced his selection of Robert M. Bonin as first assistant attorney general, Bellotti referred to it as the "first step in implementing my policy of achieving a full-time professional legal staff of superior ability."[47] He appeared to have chosen wisely. Bonin was largely unknown outside a small legal circle, but he was a very talented lawyer highly regarded by his peers. "We needed a guy who was very bright," recalled Bellotti. This was going to be a "legal job, not a political job. I said he was the smartest guy I ever met [but] he was totally non-political—useless politically."[48] The press quickly applauded Bellotti's appointment, declaring Bonin a "top flight first assistant" and a "non-political lawyer with the reputation of being careful and methodical."[49] At age forty-three, Robert Bonin was a young man on the move, the future a bright and promising place.

CHAPTER 3

The Battle for Court Reform

W HEN MICHAEL DUKAKIS became governor of Massachusetts in January 1975, it seemed to many the culmination of a long struggle on the part of progressive reformers to push the state's political system away from its ancient, entrenched cronyism, and to embrace a more inclusive politics worthy of the liberal Bay State. The new governor would move on to a remarkable career as Massachusetts' longest serving chief executive and, in 1988, as the Democratic Party's nominee for President.

Dukakis had come into office with a desire to shake up Beacon Hill by identifying and fixing stubborn, systemic problems in the executive and judicial branches. The governor, famous for hosting brown bag lunches in his office and riding the public transit system to work, was a political persona unlike any that had come before him in Massachusetts politics. He was treated with open disdain by many members of the political establishment, who simply did not understand the kind of politics represented by Dukakis, and who resented and objected to many of his efforts to change the status quo.[50] Dukakis was determined, he said in his inaugural address, to rid the state of a "patronage system that has plagued the state for decades."[51]

This was not mere rhetoric. Dukakis excluded his campaign workers from state jobs almost across the board. Said one observer: "That's how rigid he was in those days—their participation in the campaign foreclosed their participation in government."[52] His chief secretary, the person whose responsibility was to act as a clearinghouse for potential new hires in the administration, complained that "if you were even close to [the governor] it ruled you out for so many things. No patronage, no appearance of patronage—god, it was so hard to meet."[53] This standard led to strained relationships with many people who had given Dukakis political support over the years.[54]

If Michael Dukakis would break with long time friends over patronage, it should have come as no surprise that he was willing to upset other people's apple carts in order to achieve the governmental reforms he cared so deeply about. Dukakis brought a number of reform initiatives to office—ranging from the significant (the creation of an independent judicial nominating commission to professionalize the selection of judges) to the small-bore (refusing to follow the tradition of handing out low number license plates to political supporters) to the highly controversial. The governor's commitment to implementing a system wide reform of the state's court system fell into that latter category. Dukakis, a lawyer by profession, was keenly aware of serious problems plaguing the state's court system—problems that were threatening the prompt delivery of justice to the Commonwealth's citizens. Court reform quickly became a priority for the new administration.

Dukakis signaled the importance he attached to this initiative by appointing Harvard Law School Professor Archibald Cox to lead his court reform commission. Cox had recently gained national fame as the short-lived independent prosecutor in the Watergate scandal, fired by Richard Nixon as part of the infamous "Saturday night massacre." If Cox had stood up to a president, he would surely stand up to the state's entrenched legal and judicial hierarchy. Cox's appointment meant that Dukakis was serious about developing and implementing a meaningful court reform program.

The new attorney general supported Dukakis in this effort. Frank Bellotti's libertarian instincts and years of experience as a criminal defense attorney made him an early and consistent supporter of court reform. This was good news for Dukakis, who would need all the help he could get in his efforts to reform the court system.

Court reform was designed to take a poorly organized and highly politicized court system and make it more efficient. Courts were overburdened, and they were ruled by a close knit group of judges and administrators who would not tolerate any intrusion into the world they controlled with often absolute power. Massachusetts courts in the 1970s operated as a balkanized collection of fiefdoms, sustained by 417 separate and uncoordinated budgets, "each subject to the patronage and back-scratching that had given Massachusetts such a bad name in the fifties and sixties."[55] Although the state's highest court—the Supreme Judicial Court (SJC)—was highly regarded, the trial court system, anchored by the Superior Court, was generally recognized as an inefficient patronage haven. Centralizing authority in a strong chief administrative justice threatened and undermined the political and personal relationships that provided grist for the judicial mill. "It was perfectly obvious," recalled Dukakis, "that we were dealing with a nineteenth-century animal here."[56]

The final Cox Committee report did not mince words. It warned, "The administration of justice in Massachusetts stands on the brink of disaster."[57] Delays and inefficiencies in the Superior Court had "reached major proportions," giving Massachusetts the distinction of having six of the twelve most congested county court systems in the nation.[58] The committee's recommendations were designed to streamline and make more efficient the notoriously slow workings of the trial court system in part by merging the Probate, Juvenile, Housing and Land Courts within the Superior Court, and by making the new chief justice of the Superior Court a more powerful administrator. The report observed that "The simple step of vesting in one judge the continuing administrative responsibility for all matters affecting the flow of business in the Superior Court in each county would bring much improvement."[59] This new chief justice would have unprecedented and generally unlimited powers over the assignment of judges.

Much was at stake. Cox had warned in his report that if the Commonwealth failed to reorganize the judicial system, a "breakdown of justice" was imminent. But the legal and judicial establishments were having none of it. The committee's recommendations threatened business as usual and were not generally welcome in the legal community. Harvey Silverglate, whose criminal defense and civil liberties practice had thrust him to the forefront of Boston's trial bar, recalled that the entrenched powers "viewed Cox as an enemy—a Yankee, and a Harvard professor who didn't practice much. They viewed it as shaking up the comfortable little game they had going."[60]

The Judicial Council of Massachusetts, comprised of judges representing the various courts of the Commonwealth, rejected the Cox Committee findings outright. "We do not believe that the enactment of reorganization legislation will prove to be a panacea for all the ailments of the judicial system," they wrote in their 1977 report.[61] As a direct rebuttal to the Cox report, they warned their readers to "Beware Brinksmanship," opposing Cox's observation that the administration of justice stood "on the brink of disaster," and declaring that "a judicial system which has been in existence since 1620 … should not be needlessly subjected to any sudden or drastic changes or experiments."[62]

Leading jurists and lawyers also lined up to oppose the Cox Committee. Francis Poitrast, the presiding justice of the Boston

Juvenile Court and leader of the State Judicial Association, authored an op-ed piece for the *Boston Globe* entitled "Court reform vs. the children," in which he argued that the reform recommendations would harm the children who came before his court because judges would be compelled to devote time to other matters. Judge Poitrast characterized court reform as "radical" and "disastrous."[63] Thomas Burns, Chairman of the Joint Bar Association Committee on Judicial Nominations and "one of the state's most active trial lawyers" referred to the Cox Committee recommendations as "administrative flimflam and legal hokum."[64]

One of the central recommendations of the Cox Committee, that the new chief justice serve primarily as an administrator, was considered by the "working judges ... [as] a waste of judicial time and talent."[65] Some of the harshest criticism came from the outgoing Superior Court chief justice, Walter H. McLaughlin. McLaughlin was identified in the *Boston Globe* as "one of the unseen hands behind the slashing, anti-Cox Committee report which will be filed with the Judicial Council."[66]

Walter McLaughlin was not a man to be trifled with. He was a lion of the Massachusetts bar, a person of strong ambition

Figure 4: "A Hard Guy, A Tough Guy"
Superior Court Chief Justice Walter McLaughlin, Sr.

and overwhelming self-confidence. He was from a large and prominent Cambridge family, one of nine children who were known for their fierce loyalty and ambition.[67] McLaughlin's own judicial career was marked by a rapid rise. Although he did not ascend to the bench until age sixty, McLaughlin was named Superior Court chief justice a mere three years later. He was an insider's insider, a man viewed by trial lawyer Harvey Silverglate as "untouchable," and who Frank Bellotti—no pushover himself—described as "a hard guy, a tough guy."[68]

Bellotti himself, in the years before his election as attorney general, tried a murder case before McLaughlin. Bellotti's client was a man accused of murdering a young woman on the Charles River Esplanade. After a long trial the sentence was reduced from first-degree to second-degree murder. When the family of the young female victim took exception to the sentence, Bellotti recalled McLaughlin intoning from the bench: "no one told your daughter to go walking late at night along the Esplanade." Bellotti recalled wishing he could hide under the table he was sitting at.[69]

McLaughlin was leaving office reluctantly. At age seventy, he faced the uncompromising operation of the state's new mandatory retirement law. McLaughlin saw little of value in the Cox Committee recommendations and was adamant in his verdict that the central components of the Cox Committee recommendations were misplaced. McLaughlin never relented on this view. Fifteen years after leaving office, McLaughlin continued to rail against the Cox Committee recommendations. "It hasn't worked," said the long retired chief justice. "It's been a tremendous failure."[70]

McLaughlin may have had policy differences with the Cox Committee, but he also believed that the Cox Committee report reflected poorly on his administrative abilities and left a stained record of accomplishment as the final word on his tenure in office. "Any reform implied that he [McLaughlin] was doing a lousy job," recalled Judge Dermot Meagher.[71] Indeed, the report identified as a major problem the "failure to modernize the procedures and practices which govern the flow of cases," noting that "even under the present outdated organization, there is much the courts themselves can do to expedite the flow of judicial business in the trial courts and to reduce the inconvenience suffered by jurors, parties, attorneys and witnesses."[72] In an article in the *Massachusetts Law Quarterly,* Cox had written that "the absence of effective management is a primary cause of delay and inefficiency," and although he went out of his way to explain that the "fault is not personal," the clear inference was that McLaughlin had not done enough to use his substantial political influence and existing powers to improve the situation.[73] The *Boston Globe's* editorial cartoonist caricatured the old chief, surrounded by cobwebs, urging others to move ahead slowly on reform.[74]

No one doubted that McLaughlin's skills as a trial lawyer, and later a trial judge, were formidable. He was singled out by the state's Supreme Judicial Court for his skillful handling of a high profile trial for the murder of a Boston police officer.[75] The question was never McLaughlin's competence as a lawyer or a judge. But these talents did not easily transfer to the ability to move the trial court system into a more modern era, which required a different skill set. In this respect, McLaughlin was found wanting.

To his credit, Dukakis did not let McLaughlin's power and influence, or the controversial nature of court reform, deter him from moving ahead with implementing its recommendations a year before seeking re-election. "I didn't have any bone to pick necessarily with McLaughlin," said Dukakis, "I was far more interested in the whole systemic thing."[76] Dukakis wanted court reform, and intended to choose a new chief justice who would carry out the basic template of the committee recommendations.

With McLaughlin facing retirement, and the Cox Committee recommendations open for legislative debate and action, replacing the outgoing chief justice with a court reform supporter loomed large on Dukakis's agenda. McLaughlin's own choice as a successor, Superior Court Justice James P. Lynch, was a member of the Cox Committee and the only committee member who was recorded in opposition to the recommendation that the Probate, Housing, Juvenile and Land courts be consolidated within the Superior Court.[77] Lynch's opposition to one of the central recommendations of the report reflected the view of many of the incumbent judges that court reform threatened their world, and it disqualified the otherwise able jurist for consideration by the reform minded governor.

Aware of the strong bonds among many of the Superior Court justices, and the supposedly independent prosecutors who appeared before them on a daily basis, Dukakis decided to look outside the court for a possible successor to McLaughlin.[78] "I certainly wanted somebody who was strongly committed to change. And to reform. And who would implement it," said Dukakis.[79]

Choosing the new chief justice of the Superior Court was a significant opportunity for Dukakis—it would enable him to put a reform minded jurist in the midst of an anti-reform organization and it would send a signal to all that he meant business. But any new chief justice would have to deal with an entrenched bureaucracy that had grown accustomed to particular ways of doing business in the state's courtrooms. In particular, a new chief justice would have to deal with the often cozy and inappropriate relationships between the judiciary and the state's elected prosecutors—the district attorneys.

Each Massachusetts county elected a district attorney— its chief law enforcement officer, primarily responsible for criminal prosecutions. In Boston, Chief Justice McLaughlin had developed a warm working relationship with Suffolk County District Attorney Garrett Byrne. The two men were more than friends and allies—they were respected and venerable leaders of a generation of men who had participated in and led the state's legal and political systems in the 1950s and 1960s. When Garrett Byrne wanted a particular judge assigned to a case, he needed only to have a private conversation with McLaughlin, and the assignment was made. Harvey Silverglate recalled learning that McLaughlin had "almost daily *ex parte*

contact" with Byrne's chief assistant, John Gaffney.[80] These
men saw nothing wrong in their private manipulation of the
supposedly objective wheels of justice—they shared a common
sense of right and wrong, and an unspoken belief that they had
earned the ability to administer their respective offices by rules
of their own making.

In 1977 the oldest of the old guard, the winner of Boston's
political longevity prize, was Suffolk County District Attorney
Garrett Byrne. A man whose career spanned most of the century
and who epitomized the city's entrenched politics, Byrne was
personally close to many of the judges who doled out justice
from the Suffolk County courtrooms, and he had built a vast
network of political allies through years by a strategic and
persistent use of patronage. It was no coincidence that many
judges had children working as assistant district attorneys in
Byrne's office. Above all else, Byrne was a protector of the
political status quo—he had been ever since taking control
over the DA's office in 1952. Byrne and McLaughlin would
make a formidable team to frustrate Dukakis's ambitious court
reform plans.

Garrett Byrne had been district attorney of Suffolk County
for nearly a quarter century, and for nineteen years before

that he was an assistant district attorney in the same office. His political career was a window on Boston politics through most of the twentieth century. Law enforcement was his life, as was politics, and on more than one occasion Garrett Byrne demonstrated a keen understanding of public relations and the value of the dramatic public act. So deeply associated was Byrne to the image of law and order that he was referred to by the name of a popular radio program of the 1940s that featured a crime fighting hero who made city streets safe from petty thieves, gangsters and hoodlums. Garrett Byrne was "Mr. District Attorney."[81]

PART TWO

Garrett Byrne and His Times

H E WAS EIGHTY-SEVEN YEARS old, in good health and sharp as ever. The former district attorney of Suffolk County, a reticent and quiet man by nature, was the focus of attention on this June evening in 1984.[82] The occasion was the sixtieth anniversary of his graduation from Suffolk University Law School and the creation of a scholarship fund in his name.[83] The ruling classes of Boston's political and legal worlds were assembled to honor him. House Speaker Thomas "Tip" O'Neill was present, as were two other political leaders who had worked as assistants to the district attorney prior to seeking elective office—United States Senator Edward Kennedy and Boston Mayor Kevin White. For many in the crowded room, it was a time to reminisce, to recall past glories, to reflect upon the passage of time, and to marvel at the longevity of Garrett H. Byrne.

Garrett Byrne had been out of office since 1978, and it

was not a gentle exit from political life. In a bruising battle with Newman Flanagan, one of his closest protégés and a man he once referred to as having been "like a son" to him, Byrne suffered what was only his second electoral defeat in a career that began when Calvin Coolidge was president.[84] The loss may have hurt, but it did not defeat the old man. When it was his time to speak to the crowd assembled in his honor, he did so briefly and with humor. "Although I'm eighty-seven now," he said, "a young man who once worked for me came up to me the other day and said to me that he had a great stock tip for me. 'Put your money into the stock because it's going to triple in a year,' he told me. I looked at him for a moment and then told him that I don't even buy green bananas anymore."[85]

Garrett Byrne did not loom large over Boston politics. He possessed neither O'Neill's power and gregariousness nor White's fulsome mind nor Kennedy's charisma. Yet Garrett Byrne inhabited Boston's political world in as comfortable, successful and intimate a way as any man of his time. He was a skillful practitioner of the political arts, a man who understood the power of patronage, the importance of the bold headline, and the value of a political favor. In 1959, when the underdog register of probate, John Collins, was locked in a tight battle for mayor against the formidable president of the Senate, John E. Powers, it was one of Byrne's trusted staff members who brought Collins a photograph of a police bust of bookie joints in East Boston, seedy gaming parlors prominently displaying large "Powers for Mayor" signs. Collins used the photographs as evidence that Powers was "the darling of the mob," and went on to beat Powers in all but two of the city's wards.[86] Those were the kind of favors a politician didn't forget.[87]

Byrne's public service was notable for its longevity and for its conservatism. In a political career spanning a half-century he took a political risk only once. After losing a close race for a county seat early in his career, Byrne embarked on a conventional, low risk pathway that was the envy of many of his peers. He was a cautious and careful practitioner of retail politics—the kind of politics that put as much emphasis on personal loyalty and the dispensation of patronage as it did on public service. Byrne grew steadily into a leader of Boston's old boy network—a collection of men in their sixties and seventies who ruled Boston in the 1960s and 1970s. When young political reformers like Michael Dukakis and Frank Bellotti emerged to become leaders of post-JFK Massachusetts, the clash with Byrne and his peers was inevitable.

If the essence of any public man may be illuminated by his times and his surroundings, then in order to know Garrett Byrne and the conservative political establishment he came to represent, one must also know Boston—not the fresh, vital "New Boston" of the last quarter of the twentieth century, but the gritty metropolis of Byrne's youth, the Boston of 1924, a place of immigrants and a Brahmin ruling class in eclipse. Garrett Byrne's Boston was a harsh, insular, fiercely ethnic and decidedly Roman Catholic place.

CHAPTER 1

Garrett Byrne's Boston

G ARRETT BYRNE BEGAN HIS political life when he
graduated from Suffolk University's law school in
1924 and immediately stood for election to one of two state
representative seats from Boston's Ward 12. Why politics? The
prestigious law firms were small enclaves of Harvard-educated
Boston Brahmins. For a young Irish American educated in the
law, a successful career in government meant a network of loyal
friends and a lifetime's security, but it was not an easy path.
It meant a life in a rough and tumble world, where only the
savviest were fit for survival.

The master of political survival in 1924 was fifty-year-
old James Michael Curley, nearing the end of his second
term as mayor. Forbidden by law to succeed himself, Curley
had embarked on what would ultimately be an unsuccessful
campaign for governor. Although remembered largely as a
caricature of early twentieth-century Irish urban politics, Curley

was an important transitional figure—a politician with unique skills and foresight who served as a bridge between the original ward bosses, who were content for complete dominance in a narrow sphere, and their progeny, best represented by John F. Kennedy, grandson of the boss of the North End, who brought the same killer political instincts, refined by time, money and education, to a national stage.

The city he led in 1924 was, like Curley himself, in transition. Sailing into the harbor, one encountered a port at the beginning of decline. Boston's glory days as headquarters for the Cunard line and home to Donald MacKay's shipworks had faded into memory. New York had decisively supplanted Boston as the destination of choice for travelers and trade. Nevertheless, the harbor was busy, filled with a large fishing fleet and the ferries that were the only mode of transport between the downtown and East Boston, because there were no harbor tunnel or bridge crossings (the Sumner Tunnel would be opened ten years later). Boston's tallest building was the Custom House, a sixteen-story landmark near the harbor. Newspaper advertisements promoted a new household convenience: electric refrigeration—*"Let electricity take the place of ice!"* Flight was still in its infancy, and of sufficient novelty to attract crowds whenever a new aviation feat was taking place. In September, fifty thousand people crowded the airfield in East Boston to greet the Globe Fliers—American aviators who had left Santa Monica, California on March 17 to begin a trans-global adventure.[88]

Politics was also in transition. In 1924 Mayor Curley tested a portable radio broadcasting device, demonstrating his skill at moving with the times to promote himself. Martin Lomasney, the fading boss of Ward 8, continued his practice of election-eve rallies, but this year "women were present for the first time . . . and the old political campaigner did not take off his coat, collar and necktie."[89]

There were other transitions. On July 17, 1924, Isabella Stewart Gardner, aged eighty-five, died in her Italianate villa in Boston's Fenway, leaving behind a legacy for social grace and cultural eminence that has been left unsurpassed to this day. When she lived on Beacon Street, she was known to dress her windows "with an almost constantly changing parade of floral arrangements," and was so taken by the "gratitude in the faces of the passers-by … that she never for a moment considered it anything but her bounded duty to continue it faithfully."[90] "Mrs. Jack" was an important patron of the arts, befriending the likes of Paderewski, Santayana and John Singer Sargent (who twice painted her portrait).[91] Gardner was an important link to the European world of art and music, and she fashioned her Fenway residence as a shrine to her journeys abroad. Her taste in people and places was avant-garde for her times—"bohemian" in the phrase of a biographer—and her presence was so large that she became, especially after her husband's death, an important figure in the city's sense of itself: stylish, cultured, pushing the limits of inventiveness. She represented the best in Boston's cultural leadership, the kind of leadership demonstrated so grandly by other privileged Bostonians—Henry Lee Higginson, who founded the Boston Symphony Orchestra and helped finance the construction of Symphony Hall, James Jackson Storrow and his wife, Helen Osborne Storrow, whose civic and financial contributions made the Charles River Esplanade a reality, and Mary Hemenway, who saved the Old South Meeting House with a personal donation to preserve Boston's second oldest church.

If Mrs. Jack was a pillar of Boston society, Henry Cabot Lodge was the foundation of the state's Republican political establishment. Lodge, who also died in 1924, was the son of a successful merchant who made a fortune in the China trade. Educated at Harvard, Lodge was Boston blue blood to the core.[92] Lodge began his career as a reformer, allied with Theodore Roosevelt to wrest control of the national Republican Party from leaders they saw as needlessly and dangerously corrupt, but he is perhaps best remembered as a staunch isolationist and the incorrigible partisan who helped break Woodrow Wilson's health and legacy by leading the congressional opposition to the League of Nations.

Lodge first took office as a United States senator in 1893, and he quickly established for himself the role of careful guardian of "American" values. As a member of Boston's Immigration Restriction League, Lodge viewed many European immigrants as representing "lower races of less social efficiency and less moral force."[93] He had little use for the Irish and other newcomers who were now ruling Boston, and the feeling was mutual. Lodge, well known for his "cool and distant manner," was "cordially hated" by most city Democrats.[94] When he died on November 9, he was mourned by his Brahmin brethren as one of the last politically powerful Yankees, a stalwart conservative who never read an anti-immigration bill he didn't like.

The passing of Lodge and Gardner epitomized the passing of an era. The Boston of the nineteenth century was fading away, a place of genteel elegance, of black-tie dinners served by

Irish waiters, of quiet reading rooms in private clubs built by Irish laborers, of grand public buildings like the State House, a gold-crested jewel atop the city's most exclusive and prestigious neighborhood, its interior a marble masterpiece whose mosaic tile floors were laid by Italian immigrant craftsmen and scrubbed by Irish cleaning women. Boston in 1924 was a different place—a teeming metropolis ruled by the fiercely ethnic and decidedly Catholic children of immigrants.

Like most of the great East Coast American cities, Boston grew from a colonial town into a great urban center largely on the strength of the influx of thousands of European immigrants. By 1924, foreign stock comprised more than fifty percent of Boston's population, but one group of immigrants stood out. Of all the people who made their way to Boston seeking a better life, none were to dominate the city more completely and for so long than the Irish.

It is a story that has often been told: in Ireland in the decade from 1841 to 1851, as an unprecedented famine deprived its people of the important dietary staples they depended on, nearly one million people died from disease related to malnutrition. At any one time, nearly half a million men were without work of any kind.[95] The natural response—indeed, the prudent thing to do—was to leave the land that had failed them. The great flight from famine led to many different places, but America was a chief destination and Boston, as one of the most important ports of the day, a chief place of debarkation. Now in 1924, the children and grandchildren of these Irish immigrants dominated the city, by virtue of the sheer magnitude of their population, and because they had struggled to achieve power in the political arena and had won.

The Irish brought many elements of their culture with them to Boston, and their strong connection with Roman Catholicism was a central element of their lives—one that sustained them in hard times, and offered them hope when life was doling out little but despair. As devout Catholics, many of the Irish looked to the church hierarchy for guidance and direction. Looming over the city as a brooding and powerful presence in 1924 was Boston's first cardinal, a man of overwhelming arrogance and questionable ethics, of strong ambition and equally strong temper, who imposed an uncompromising conservative orthodoxy on his flock.

William Cardinal O'Connell had no personal roots in Boston. He was born and raised in the northern Massachusetts mill town of Lowell, and received his clerical training in Rome.

Boston was his means to power and nothing more. O'Connell made no secret of his desire to escape the city as often as he could. His many excursions to the Bahamas (he would spend three months a year there on vacation) and to Europe earned him the moniker "Gangplank Bill." He removed himself literally and figuratively from contact with the urban poor by abandoning the church's headquarters in the then squalid South End for the more refined outer precincts of Boston, where he conducted the business of the Archdiocese from the gentle and secluded hills of Brighton, which he likened to the Palatine Hills of Rome.[96]

The Cardinal saw no need to stand clear of local politics. Rather he immersed himself in it.[97] O'Connell's brand of conservative orthodoxy expressed itself in the political debate in many ways: opposition to laws banning child labor, opposition to a state run lottery, and opposition to proposals that would liberalize the sale of contraceptives.[98] The Cardinal's power expressed itself most famously when he persuaded Mayor John Fitzgerald to send his daughter Rose to a convent school rather than Wellesley College—a decision that Rose Fitzgerald Kennedy would remember, decades later and (remarkably) after years of overwhelming personal tragedy, as her "greatest regret."[99]

O'Connell would brook no objection from the city's civil authorities, and could cow even the strong willed Curley into compliance with his own views. When Curley deigned to support a referendum that would ban child labor O'Connell, who opposed the child labor reforms of this era because they interfered with what the Cardinal believed were the sole and exclusive decision making rights of parents, directed his parish priests to take to the pulpit and excoriate Curley. In a moment reminiscent of Pope Gregory VII compelling Emperor Henry IV to kneel before him in the snow at Canossa, it did not take more than twenty-four hours for Curley to bow to the Cardinal's opinion and reverse his opinion.[100]

The Cardinal's influence was felt well beyond the halls and corridors of the State House and City Hall. He was the city's primary moral arbiter, weighing in against what he termed the "dangers of corruption in the growing generation."[101] O'Connell took public issue with many works of literature and railed against Hollywood's "unutterably filthy plots." In 1923 he participated in a community protest against the local production of Richard Strauss's opera *Salome*.[102] Ironically, the man who had once exclaimed with pride that "the Puritan has passed, the Catholic remains," was himself instituting subjective moral standards that would have been the pride of John Winthrop's Puritan Boston.

This was Boston in 1924: a place in transition, a place in decline, a place where the moral primacy of the Catholic Church trumped the strongest of politicians. This was Garrett Byrne's Boston—the place in which Byrne cut his political teeth, the people and events that helped shape the views and instincts of this young man who would now take his first step onto the political stage, and who would be a player long after most of his contemporaries had faded from memory. It was a difficult and dark place, a vibrant, gritty metropolis so strikingly described by Thomas Wolfe approaching the city by train in 1920 on his way from North Carolina to Harvard University: Boston, "the enchanted city, the approach so smoky, blind and stifled, to the ancient web, the old grimed thrilling barricades of Boston ... bitterly, bitterly Boston, one time more."[103]

Seeking election to the state Legislature in 1924, the twenty-seven-year-old Garrett Byrne emerged out of a political tradition that feared and respected the Catholic hierarchy, that nurtured the politically connected, the wise-guy and the knave, and that above all prized loyalty to one's peers.[104] Political leaders steeped in this tradition, as *Boston Globe* reporter Renee Loth wrote, lived in a world where "quid pro quo was as familiar an expression as any in Sunday's Latin Mass."[105] Characterization as a political insider was a matter of distinction in a city where James Michael Curley was a cultural hero and felicity to one's ethnic brethren was an article of faith. The political and legal worlds of Boston came together in an area confined by the dark and narrow streets and alleys that connected City Hall to the courthouse at Pemberton Square and, further up Beacon Hill, to the State House.

It was here that Garrett Byrne got his start.

CHAPTER 2

Entering the Fray

I N HIS NINETY-FIRST YEAR, Garrett Byrne recalled to his longtime trusted friend Lawrence Cameron that, as a young man and political novice, he had been very active in the Roxbury Tammany Club—the club founded and led by James Michael Curley. Byrne knew that you needed Curley's blessing to run for state Legislature, but was rebuffed when he sought it in 1924. "Aren't you premature?" Curley asked Byrne.[106] But Byrne would not be called off the race, and he went ahead with a vigorous campaign.

1924 was a raucous election year. Politics in those days was practiced "realistically, ruthlessly, and with an eye toward ultimate success rather than to ideals and ethics."[107] The *Boston Globe* reported that at one political rally, the crowd broke into factions "and began a battle with sticks, stones, bottles and even paving bricks."[108] On primary election day Garrett Byrne received the second highest vote in his district, 2,055 votes to

Patrick J. Sullivan's 2,479.[109] In those times, each district sent two legislators to the Massachusetts House of Representatives. Byrne's strong second place finish meant that he had won one of the two Democratic nominations and, in increasingly Democratic Boston, his election was assured.

Garrett Byrne's ambition burned steadily but not brightly. His political aspirations were modest. Personal and political security were apparently his chief goals. How else to explain his decision, as a young and successful politician, and after only two terms in the state Legislature, to seek county-wide office as register of deeds, a low profile county seat where officeholders could rely on political obscurity and longevity?

Byrne waged a serious campaign to unseat the incumbent register, William T. A. Fitzgerald in 1928. Byrne opened his campaign in Charlestown's City Square, and commenced with an aggressive campaign during which he questioned Fitzgerald's party loyalty.[110] Fitzgerald refused to take the bait and stuck to a tried and true formula, reminding voters of his "faithful service and loyalty to your interests."[111] After waging a vigorous campaign, it became clear on election night that Byrne's effort would fall short of the mark.[112]

The final tally was 48,666 for Fitzgerald to Byrne's 40,132.

Although Byrne had carried only six of Boston's twenty-two wards, and none of the other communities which comprise Suffolk County, his vote was respectable.[113] He was out but not finished, and he learned an important lesson about political survival. He would not oppose the established order again. He could survive to another day, especially if he cut the right deal.

That day came in 1933, the year Garrett Byrne set the course for his lengthy career. Nineteen hundred thirty-three was an election year in Boston, and the incumbent mayor—once again, James Michael Curley—was, according to law, ineligible to run for re-election. Curley was approaching the apex of his career, and he wanted to have some continuing measure of control over city government as he once again set his sights on the governor's office –a race he lost in 1924 but would win in 1934. That control would come from a compliant mayoral candidate, someone who could be a legitimate candidate in his own right but who would owe election and allegiance to Curley.

Curley found his man in the district attorney of Suffolk County, William J. Foley of South Boston. It was no matter that Curley had previously referred to the district attorney as the "dumb Dora of Pemberton Square," for it was not Foley's

IQ that qualified him for Curley's support.[114] It was his ability to put together a winning coalition that counted. And on paper at least, with populous South Boston as a base, Foley looked like a strong mayoral candidate.

Foley and Curley needed all the help they could get to win the election. At the same time, Garrett Byrne was available for an opportunity to re-enter politics, perhaps one that offered job security. In an election where District Attorney Foley would *still* be district attorney if he lost, Garrett Byrne found what he was looking for. The principals are all dead, and the discrete confidences of their political understandings have gone with them to their respective graves, but one can reasonably surmise that Byrne, a proven vote getter and popular local figure, made his bargain. Could Byrne deliver important votes to Foley's coalition? Did he offer his unqualified support for a chance to serve in the district attorney's office? The public record only invites speculation, but Byrne did support Foley and Foley did appoint him as an assistant district attorney for Suffolk County prior to the election for mayor in 1933.

At least one chronicler posits that Curley did not like Foley and supported the DA's bid with reluctance.[115] It may be true that Curley disdained Foley, but contemporary press accounts reveal a Curley genuinely engaged in Foley's campaign.[116] The *Boston Globe* reported that "There can be no doubt about Mayor Curley's influence. He has many enthusiastic friends and it is said he has swung to Mr. Foley city employees who had intended to vote for [former mayor] Malcolm Nichols."[117]

These were times when this year's ally was next year's enemy—volatile times marked by a political revolving door of allegiances suited to the peculiar needs of the day.[118] Whatever Curley's true feelings (if he could be said to have had feelings when it came to politics), it is reasonable to conclude that in 1933 he forged a political marriage of convenience among himself, Foley, Byrne and others.[119] The leading candidate for mayor that year was Frederick W. Mansfield, an old Curley foe and close associate of the Cardinal, who was famously described as "spectacular as a four-day-old codfish and as colorful as a lump of mud."[120] As election day drew near, Foley declared that he would win by a fifty-thousand-vote plurality.[121] On election eve, the ever-wily Curley charged that Mansfield was planning election day dirty tricks at Foley's expense. "I am exposing it in advance," said Curley, "Mansfield could have as many repeaters (citizens attempting to vote more than once using different names) as bootleggers in Boston, and [even] then could not get in."[122]

In the end, Foley's South Boston base and Curley's city-wide machinations were not enough. Foley lost badly, placing third behind former Mayor Nichols.[123] Foley even finished a distant third in Garrett Byrne's Ward 12, reflecting the citywide trend.[124] On election night Foley congratulated Mansfield with a short concession statement.[125] He would try again for the mayoralty in 1937, unsuccessfully, but he remained a popular district attorney and he would remain in that post until the first of December 1952, when his wife found him dead on the bathroom floor in their South Boston home.[126] He was sixty-five years old.

It was Foley's final—and ultimate—accommodation to Garrett Byrne.

CHAPTER 3

Business as Usual

F OLEY'S DEATH HAD come as "a profound shock to the community" and created a huge political opportunity—whoever was appointed district attorney of Suffolk County would have at his disposal an engine of patronage second only to Boston's mayor.[127] Outgoing Governor Paul Dever, a Democrat, would decide who would replace Foley for the remainder of the deceased district attorney's unexpired four-year term. A variety of players immediately began to jockey for position. The attorney general named one of his assistants, Timothy Murphy, as interim district attorney.[128] But the governor would have the final word, and Paul Dever and Garrett Byrne were close personal friends.[129]

"Byrne will be given the position if he wants it," reported the *Boston Herald* the day after Foley's death.[130] The conventional political wisdom was that if Governor Dever attempted a political comeback in 1954, "Byrne's occupancy of this key political post will serve in the nature of an insurance policy."[131] The *Herald*, Boston's newspaper of record in the 1950s, castigated the late district attorney as having "a do-nothing or a do-as-little-as-possible philosophy which threatened at times to produce a scandal," and called on the governor to appoint "a crusading district attorney."[132] But it was not to be.

On December 17, 1952, a reticent, balding fifty-five-year-old, described as "husky" by one reporter, was appointed to complete the two years remaining on Foley's term.[133] Garrett Byrne was, by appearance, an unlikely crime fighter. Predictably he pledged to maintain the status quo, referring to Foley as "one of the greatest men I have ever known," and declaring: "There will be no firings by me."[134]

The *Globe* damned the new DA with faint praise, noting the likelihood that he would "conduct the office in the spirit of his predecessor."[135] The *Herald* was less charitable, noting that "The voices of evil come in many inflections... They want things left alone. The status quo. Business as usual."[136]

He had waited patiently as Foley's assistant for nineteen years. Now by accident, by sheer force of luck and longevity, he was district attorney. In order to keep the job, he would have to earn it. Garrett Byrne was up for election to a full term as district attorney in September 1954. He would have to prove himself to the voters and to the strange mix of media and political wise guys who helped formulate public opinion.

Byrne had not faced the voters since 1928, and had not won an election since 1926. He was unknown and untested but he knew what he needed to do to win election as district attorney in his own right in 1954. The challenge was daunting. The candidates included the son and namesake of the popular former district attorney, William Foley, Jr., and the man who served ever so briefly as interim district attorney in the three weeks between Foley's death and Byrne's appointment, Timothy Murphy.

If Byrne was Foley's protégé he was also Curley's political descendant. Byrne understood that he needed to capture the public imagination, stay in the public eye, and portray himself as a vigorous, tough, effective prosecutor. His solid political instincts, combined with the remarkable good luck that followed him through most of his career, made him a formidable candidate. And on this occasion, at this crucial moment in his public life, Garrett Byrne did not falter or stumble. He rose to the occasion with an impressive display of political savvy.

He began his pre-election media campaign with a probe of debt-pooling firms that made front-page news for several days in late August 1954. But this mini-scandal was small beer compared to the political fortune that awaited him. On August 29, 1954, news broke of the escape of an inmate from the Charles Street Jail. This was no ordinary inmate. The escaped prisoner was Elmer "Trigger" Burke, a "murder-for-hire" man who had made a spectacularly unsuccessful attempt to kill Joseph J. "Specs" O'Keefe, the mastermind of the Brink's robbery and the government's chief witness in the developing investigation of that legendary theft.[137]

Burke had passed through four locked gates at the prison "like a ghost." Three masked men aided Burke in his escape.[138] The escapee—referred to by the press as a "kill-crazy psychopath"—was described as "short, wiry and mean of eye" with "an utter disdain for the law" and a "craftiness akin to that of an animal."[139] No Hollywood script writer could portray a villain more vividly, and Byrne was thrust into the role of the tough law and order man, pledged to protect the vulnerable public from this killer on the loose. The escape had all the elements of high drama, and it kept the district attorney on the front pages of the city's newspapers for thirteen consecutive days. It was an enviable position for a man seeking the votes of the citizens only days later.

To add to the drama, and cement in the public mind that this was a personal struggle between Byrne and Burke, between good and evil, Burke had the temerity to telephone the Boston police from a South Shore restaurant in order to threaten Byrne's life.[140] Burke reportedly vowed, in words that appear to have been cleansed for publication, "to foul up Garry Byrne. If I'm unlucky enough to go to trial, I'll plead guilty and that bum will lose out on a lot of good publicity. I'll take care of this 'fighting District Attorney' before I get through with him."[141] Later, another witness would quote Burke having said before his escape, "I will be out soon, and when I get out, I'll kill that Byrne."[142]

Garrett Byrne took full advantage of his opportunity. Demonstrating coolness under pressure, competence at rapid and effective criminal investigation, and toughness as a prosecutor, Byrne's conduct in the days immediately following the escape gave the strong impression of a man who had the crisis well in control. His actions were a textbook demonstration of effective law enforcement.

Byrne immediately convened a grand jury to investigate

what he termed Burke's "fantastic and unbelievable escape" from the Charles Street Jail.[143] "This brazen threat to law and order," said Byrne, "will not go unchallenged."[144] Byrne made quick work of his investigation. It was soon revealed that the chief jail officer permitted the escaped inmate to exercise a favored position in the jail yard,[145] and two part-time guards were fingered for giving Burke assistance with his escape."[146] Byrne's pursuit culminated in the indictment of eight defendants and the arrest of the chief officer of the jail and three prison guards.[147] The district attorney tantalized the press with news that there was "still more startling testimony" to be given to the grand jury, and he threatened to summons the Suffolk County sheriff himself as a witness.[148]

The *Boston Herald's* crime reporter was so impressed by Byrne's performance that, in the middle of a news account, he all but endorsed the district attorney for election:

> *This is not a plug for District Attorney Byrne who, as is well known, is a candidate for election. But those who engineered this jail delivery, and Burke, have underestimated this prosecutor's ability to get to the bottom of a serious breach of the law as this. He is very resourceful and ... has surrounded*

himself with the best investigatory brains in the Boston Police
Department, as well as some shrewd private detectives.[149]

In the midst of this frenzy of activity, with the election for district attorney scheduled for September 15, his opponents could not hope to keep pace with Byrne's prominence in the daily news. And Byrne's luck continued. For if the daily headlines of the escape of "Trigger" Burke were not enough to keep voter attention directed away from Byrne's competitors, there came in late August and early September the two great hurricanes of 1954.

The first storm, Hurricane Carol, hit on August 31, a "rampaging hurricane—the worst since 1938."[150] The death and destruction were of historic proportions: forty-seven dead and over one thousand injured.[151] WBZ Television's broadcasting tower toppled, and in a sad and sickening moment the famous steeple of the Old North Church collapsed onto the street below.[152] Eleven days later a second hurricane, Edna, battered the coast, completing the devastation of the first.[153] The public and the press were justifiably distracted from routine political news emanating from the wards and precincts of Suffolk County. And all the while four men vied for the office of district attorney.

The major candidates played to their respective strengths. Timothy Murphy, the former interim district attorney, ran as a clean cut professional, attacking Byrne for sensationalizing crime after it occurred as opposed to preventing crime in the first place. City Councilor William Foley, Jr., ran on his own considerable popularity as well as the memory of his father.[154] Foley's mother took to the air waves with a radio address, invoking her husband's memory as she appealed to the voters to help her son "carry on the tradition of his father."[155]

But Byrne was running on a solid record and he left nothing to chance. On election eve, he demonstrated his understanding of how to succeed in modern political campaigns and used the new communications medium of television in a final appeal to voters.[156] In a pre-election prediction James Michael Curley called the election for Byrne. The district attorney "has had so many opportunities in recent months and has taken advantage of them with such good judgment and skill that he, in Curley's opinion, can't be beaten," wrote a *Herald* reporter.[157] Curley, who knew a comer when he saw one, was quick to offer the support of what was left of his organization to Byrne.

When the votes were counted, Curley's prophecy came

true. Byrne defeated Foley, his nearest rival, by a two-to-one margin. This primary victory was decisive and impressive and given Suffolk County's Democratic proclivities, tantamount to election. Byrne thanked the voters for their confidence, accepting "this inspiring mandate ... to continue our war on narcotics, indecency, organized crime and all other forces seeking to destroy law and order in our community."[158] Byrne's comments suggest that he saw his position in law enforcement as one that demanded adherence to a strict moral code. His election night message was rooted in the ethics and morality of a man who seemed to believe that only he stood between the decent citizens of Suffolk County and those who would, in a variety of ways, prey upon them.

Garrett Byrne had worked hard for this victory, had waited patiently since 1933, labored in obscurity while waiting for his opportunity, and when his time came he made the most of it. This was not a victory of party or patronage or political machine. This was an intensely personal victory, won by a man who understood the rules of the emerging politics of the media age, and who played by those rules with aggressive skill. They were skills he would demonstrate often in a long career as Suffolk County district attorney.

CHAPTER 4

A Crusading District Attorney

G ARRETT BYRNE'S KNACK for the headline making, dramatic event was never more vividly on display than when he ran Cassius Clay, Sonny Liston and the world heavyweight boxing title fight out of town in the late spring of 1965.

Cassius Clay—later known as Muhammad Ali—became world heavyweight champion in February 1964 when he beat Sonny Liston in a controversial match in Miami, Florida.[159] At the time of the match Sonny Liston was under contract to Inter-Continental Promoters, Inc. Prior to the title bout, Inter-Continental signed a secret agreement with Clay mandating that, in the event he beat their man Liston, Clay's next fight would be a re-match promoted by Inter-Continental.[160] Clay, the underdog before the fight, was paid fifty thousand dollars for signing the agreement. Clay's secret contract and the manner in which he won the fight (Liston sat down on his stool and complained that his shoulder was bothering him) fueled suspicions that the heavyweight champion match was rigged.[161] Miami District Attorney Richard Gerstein, who uncovered the details of the secret pre-fight contract, found that a well-known gambler and bookmaker had visited Liston's dressing room the night of the fight, and that Liston knowingly went into the ring "with a lame or sore arm" without informing the Miami Boxing Commission of his condition.[162] A growing number of observers believed the fight was fixed.[163]

Byrne and others in Boston should have been suspicious when the agreement to hold the rematch in Boston was signed at Logan Airport on September 14, 1964. *Boston Globe* sports columnist Harold Kaese had reported that while "other reasons may be invented, the real reason Boston is in line for the rematch is that other states do not want it."[164] But Byrne did not pick up on the implications of this statement, not until much later when Gerstein briefed him on his findings from the Miami investigation. As a consequence, the result is that Byrne acted only several weeks before the title fight was to take place, and his actions took everyone by surprise. His timing and his motives were questioned by the press.

On May 5, 1965, Byrne's men went to Suffolk Superior

Court seeking to enjoin the title fight as a "public nuisance."[165] The essence of the complaint was that the fight's licensed promoter, Sam Silverman, was a front for Inter-Continental which was not licensed in Massachusetts. If true, the district attorney's allegations meant that Silverman had illegally loaned his license to Inter-Continental. More important, the allegation that Inter-Continental had "alone, on its own behalf, negotiated and completed the sale or … assignment of the so-called ancillary rights for radio, television and motion picture coverage" meant that the Commonwealth would be cheated out of its share of the lucrative ancillary rights from the fight.[166] Simply put, the real money to be made from the title bout was not the take at the gate, estimated to be nearly one half million dollars, but the television and other ancillary rights, estimated at a minimum of $4.5 million.[167]

Massachusetts law required that a promoter licensed by the State Boxing Commission must pay to the state treasurer "a sum equal to five percent of the total amount paid or to be paid for television or broadcasting rights."[168] But Silverman, not Inter-Continental, was the licensee, and Silverman's take pursuant to his contract with Inter-Continental was limited to a lump sum payment of fifteen thousand dollars.[169] There

Figure 5: The Old Guard Personified
District Attorney Garrett Byrne

was a real question whether the Commonwealth could ever successfully recover its share of the ancillary rights—some two hundred thirty thousand dollars—from Inter-Continental.

The men who promoted professional boxing in the United States were tough-minded businessmen, not to be trifled with. They made millions in an environment filled with unsavory individuals who represented the seamy side of the sport. But it was a mistake to underestimate Garrett Byrne. Yes, he was over sixty years old and "husky," and yes, he wore thick black-rimmed eyeglasses and smoked using a cigarette holder.[170] But Garrett Byrne was no pushover. And in the courtrooms of Suffolk County, his world since 1933 and his domain since 1952, Garrett Byrne was one tough customer.

It took courage for Garrett Byrne to take on the boxing world and to create an environment where Boston and the Commonwealth could lose the title fight. Inter-Continental knew this, and played its strong card almost immediately. The Clay/Liston fight was going to take place "in Boston, some other city, in a barn or on a barge," said Inter-Continental's Harold Conrad, and if Boston lost out on this event, it would be Garrett Byrne's fault.[171]

The sports writers who were covering the story started to

turn on Byrne, asking "who got Byrne thinking this way?" and questioning whether "somebody higher up put pressure on the DA?"[172] The *Boston Globe* said in an editorial that it was Byrne's timing "which is curious. Did his investigators indeed come up with some hot new information only weeks before the scheduled fight? This and related questions deserve an early public answer."[173]

Byrne was steadfast. "I want the public protected," he said. "This is the first time, yes, that any thing has been done about the fight game, but there's a lot of money in ancillary rights to protect. I want this fight run right."[174] Inter-Continental offered to put up the ancillary rights money as a bond and litigate the matter after the fight. Byrne rejected the offer and directed his men to move ahead.[175]

That was enough for Inter-Continental. Plainly wary of the scrutiny of a protracted judicial proceeding prior to the bout, they chose to change venue. On the afternoon of May 7, Inter-Continental's attorney announced that the fight was being moved from the Boston Garden to the Central Maine Youth Center in Lewiston, Maine, population 41,000.[176] Inter-Continental wanted out of Boston, out of court, and out of Garrett Byrne's line of fire. But the district attorney would not let go, responding to the news of the move by announcing a possible grand jury investigation of the entire affair.[177]

He had cost Boston and the Commonwealth over one hundred and twenty thousand dollars in taxes and at least one million dollars in business, according to one report. "Maybe Byrne is doing this town a favor," mused *Boston Globe* sports reporter Bud Collins. "But I think he has done the New Boston, which is trying to promote interest in its affairs, more harm than good."[178]

Byrne would not play the fall guy. When he finally went public with the details of his case on May 11, it was a bombshell of a story. Intimating that there may have been payoffs to Massachusetts political figures in an effort to grease the way for the bout to take place in Boston, Byrne minced few words. "The way the thing was going," he said, "I was set up to be the patsy."[179] He noted that "every other big city and state turned [the fight] down, and we come along and accept it. The real question now is why the Boxing Commission let the fight come here."[180]

He explained why he had come so late to realize that the fight should be stopped. "When they made the rematch for Boston I didn't pay much attention to it," said Byrne, but when he "broached the subject of ancillary rights [with the state's Boxing Commission] no one knew what I was talking about."[181] Byrne said that if the fight had gone forward as planned, "the Commonwealth would have been cheated out of two hundred thirty thousand dollars owed on the television and radio rights."[182]

He had no regrets, said the district attorney. "There was a stench about everything. I didn't like the fight before and I don't like it now. I make no apologies for what I did."[183] He saved his final words for the press: "And another thing, I wish they'd keep sportswriters out of court."[184]

CHAPTER 5

Abuse of Power

G ARRETT BYRNE'S successful, courageous handling of the Clay/Liston fight won him respect and recognition as a tough, honest and effective law enforcement official. In July 1965, President Lyndon Johnson appointed him to a national crime commission.[185] But as he entered what would be the final decade of his public career, Byrne began to show signs of losing the focus and the skills that had sustained him for so long. As he grew older, Byrne seemed more fixed on matters of public morals and less concerned with traditional crime fighting. By 1970, at age seventy-two, he was in many ways an anachronism, a product of the 1920s and 1930s who was not able or willing to adapt to the changing times.

The same district attorney who had gone to court to protect the citizens against rapacious promoters and a crooked fight was, in 1970, developing a case to prevent the hit Broadway play, *Hair,* from being performed in Boston.[186] This had nothing to do with protecting the public from rip-off artists or criminals. This was about Garrett Byrne's sense of public morals and decency, and the role he believed government ought to play in protecting citizens from what he viewed as offensive material. In the Boston that formed Garrett Byrne's personal and political views, government officials were properly charged with the role of public censors.

Byrne's moral sense was shaped by the city of his youth, a place where public morality was formed by the stern missions of the Watch and Ward Society and the Catholic League of Decency. Boston mayors had a long history of banning works of art, emboldened by a state statute that gave them broad powers and complete discretion to close down any entertainment in their city with which they took issue. Eugene O'Neill's play *Strange Interlude* was banned, as was Lillian Hellman's play *The Children's Hour.* Many great American novels, including Theodore Dreiser's *An American Tragedy,* John Dos Passos's *Manhattan Transfer* and Sinclair Lewis's *Elmer Gantry* were all banned from local libraries and bookstores.[187]

Those precedents were alive and well in Byrne's mind when *Hair* came to Boston. *Hair's* successful runs in New York and fourteen other cities across the country, not to mention its two hit tunes, "Aquarius" and "Let the Sun Shine In," meant nothing to him. Garrett Byrne's Boston had standards that must be met, even if it took the power of the government to do so.

Shortly after *Hair* opened at Boston's Wilbur Theater on February 22, 1970, Byrne indicated his intent to prosecute both the performers and the producers of the play. Byrne demanded that the play's local producers delete nude scenes that he believed violated the state's "open and gross lewdness" statutes.[188] The producers went to court to prevent the district attorney from taking action. "Isn't it time," asked the *Boston Globe*, "to end the 'banned in Boston' syndrome?"[191]

During an evidentiary proceeding before a single justice of the state's highest court, Clive Barnes, the drama critic for the *New York Times,* testified (in what was perhaps an exaggerated moment) that *Hair* was "artistically the most important work in American theatre since *Oklahoma.*"[189] The justices of the Supreme Judicial Court attended a performance of the play, and issued a decision that allowed the play to continue if it modified or removed certain scenes that included nudity and simulated sexual activity.[190]

These restrictions were unacceptable to the producers, who stopped the play and sought relief in federal court.

They won an important victory when, on May 6, 1970, the Federal District Court allowed the play to continue without restrictions, declaring that the First Amendment did not allow such interference with live theatrical productions. "We cannot escape the conclusion," said the court, "that to apply the standards of the street and marketplace to the world behind the footlights would be to sanction a censorship dragnet of unconstitutional proportions."[192]

Ultimately, Byrne ended up looking just a bit old fashioned and perhaps a little foolish.[193] But his efforts to close down *Hair,* and later the film *I Am Curious (Yellow),* were a matter of minor public notice compared with his decision four years later to prosecute Doctor Kenneth Edelin for murder.[194] Byrne's prosecution of Edelin in an effort to stop legal abortions in Suffolk County attracted national attention and raised questions about the fairness and the focus of Garrett Byrne's office.

Kenneth Edelin was the chief resident in obstetrics and gynecology at Boston City Hospital. He had come to Boston as a self-described thirty-two-year-old idealist, fresh from three years of experience as a general medical officer in the Air Force.[195] Edelin was highly regarded by his peers and committed to bringing quality medical services to the disenfranchised populations of the inner city.[196] The doctors at Boston City Hospital had to deal each day with difficult medical issues, made more challenging by the poverty and poor education of their patients. Many young women were victimized by a male-dominated culture that treated them as sex objects and pregnancy factories. They came to Boston City Hospital looking for help, and abortion was legal, within the limits established under *Roe v. Wade* in 1973.

The abortions and fetal tissue research projects that took place at Boston City Hospital offended conservative right-to-life groups in Massachusetts. Led by Dr. Mildred Jefferson, these anti-abortion constituencies brought an uncompromising religious perspective to the discussion. Anti-abortion activists made numerous complaints to a variety of like-minded local officials,[197] notably City Councilor Albert "Dapper" O'Neil, who conducted public hearings on the practices at City Hospital, and State Representative Raymond Flynn.[198]

While Boston's political and religious leaders debated the propriety of abortion following *Roe v. Wade,* doctors like Kenneth Edelin responded to the harsh realities faced by poor young women who had few safe places to turn to when confronted by the prospect of an unwanted pregnancy. Evonne

Gilbert (a pseudonym used by Edelin in his memoir *Broken Justice*) was seventeen years old, sixteen weeks pregnant and scared when her mother brought her to Boston City Hospital for an abortion. "I can't take her home pregnant," her mother said. "Vonnie can't come home pregnant. She can't continue this pregnancy. Her father can't know about this, Dr. Edelin."[199]

Edelin described the situation as one he had had seen many times: "Many of the women who came in for second trimester abortions were teenagers, often trying to hide their pregnancies until it was too late. Many were alone, lonely and with nowhere else to turn. There was little or no hope that the men who got them pregnant would either be fathers to or providers for the children they made."[200] With her mother's consent and support, Evonne placed herself under Edelin's care. Edelin believed that he was following all proper medical and hospital procedures, and that he was protected by *Roe v. Wade* when he performed what turned out to be a very difficult surgical abortion on Evonne.[201]

In all of his high profile prosecutions, Garrett Byrne had a villain and a victim. The villain this time was not a bank robber or a rapacious boxing promoter, it was a respected doctor. The victim was a fetus, referred to in the indictment as a "baby boy." The language of the indictment reflected the inflammatory nature of the entire case. It charged that Edelin "did assault and beat a certain person, to wit, a male child described to the said [grand] jurors as 'baby boy' and by such assault and beating did kill said person."[202] Byrne assigned the man he believed was the best trial lawyer in his office to the case—Newman Flanagan, a smart and effective prosecutor with an ebullient personality and a penchant for wearing outrageously flashy ties. For all of his outward flash, Flanagan was a hard-driving and skillful lawyer who understood Suffolk County juries as well or better than most of his peers.

Edelin hired prominent defense attorney William Homans to defend him. He was in good hands. Bill Homans was one of the giants of Boston's small but effective civil liberties bar—a hard drinking, chain smoking, meticulously prepared workaholic who took on the toughest cases and often the least appealing defendants. Homans's trial skills were formidable, and he made a strong impression on juries with his "long dark hair tinged with white at the sides, piercing dark eyes set deep in their sockets, a craggy face (once described as a "giant Apache face") and a smile both sudden and engaging."[203] Homans was initially taken aback by the indictment. "It doesn't make sense," he told Edelin. "By the law, they have virtually no case. I wonder if Garrett Byrne is getting ready for retirement…"[204]

The trial was largely a battle of semantics and a parade of conflicting expert testimony, with both sides offering very different recollections about what took place and very different opinions about the implications of Edelin's conduct.[205] Byrne was challenged for using his office in an inappropriate manner. Some saw the case "as essentially a political move in response to pressure from this city's anti-abortion forces."[206] Others noted with cynicism that the indictment "coincided with an election year in which … Byrne was running for re-election."[207] The *New York Times* criticized the "impatient prosecutors in Suffolk County" who were "asking the jury to define the crime before it decides the defendant's guilt or innocence."[208] "No matter how nobly motivated the prosecutors may consider themselves," said the *Times,* "their efforts to set social policy in a criminal courtroom constitute a gross abuse of the legal process."[209]

At the end of the trial the Suffolk County jury convicted Edelin of manslaughter. Assistant District Attorney Flanagan, having attained the conviction, did not press for a tough sentence. Edelin was sentenced to one year of probation.[210] A candlelight march and rally on Boston Common drew a large crowd of people to express their outrage over the verdict.[211] Dr. Leon White, Boston's Commissioner of Health and Hospitals, said, "I just think Edelin has been made a fall guy in an issue that should be or could be decided without damaging what I consider a very fine doctor's career."[212] The *New York Times* weighed in again after the "almost unbelievable" conviction: the case "was an attempt to use a criminal jury to set social policy … the law was being politicized. This was an exercise that should be considered intolerable in any court of law."[213] The *Boston Globe* joined the *Times* in castigating Byrne's "abuse of legal process,"[214] and the governor's wife, Kitty Dukakis, publicly referred to the verdict as "a rather sad precedent."[215]

In the end it was all a muddle. Much public energy, substantial public funds, and the best talent in the district attorney's office had been committed to a trial about public morality. The trial and conviction served only to further polarize the city on an issue that resisted easy resolution. And its conclusion provided no clarity about who was right and who was wrong. In 1976, the Massachusetts Supreme Judicial Court reversed and set aside the manslaughter verdict, stating that there was insufficient evidence to go to a jury to prove the DA's case.[216]

Garrett Byrne had authorized, sanctioned and directed the Edelin prosecution. Yet he left no lasting impression on the public. Byrne left the entire trial, and most related press statements and interviews, to Newman Flanagan. This may have been on account of his advanced age, or his trust in Flanagan, or a variety of other factors, but it meant that the headlines went to Flanagan, not Byrne. It was a significant political lapse on Byrne's part, and it would cost him dearly. For he could not know it in 1974, when he won re-election, but it would be Newman Flanagan, his able and trusted assistant, the man he referred to as being "like a son" to him, who four years later would provide him with his stiffest political challenge in over two decades.[217]

Seeking re-election in 1978, Garrett Byrne was over eighty years old, and Flanagan smelled political blood. Byrne's political longevity was certainly remarkable, but he was in 1978 a survivor, not a pioneer. In 1974, in a four-person primary, Byrne had won by an uncomfortably narrow margin.[218] He had been in office for over a quarter of a century and was increasingly dependent on his assistants for help administering the office.[219] He needed all of his political powers, all of his instinctive skills, to win re-election against his former protégé.

Byrne could still raise sufficient funds,[220] and could depend on the political support of powerful men like Mayor Kevin White.[221] But what he needed more than anything else was an issue, a cause, some defining event that would capture the imaginations of the voters and remind them that he was still their tough, honest, fighting district attorney.

Garrett Byrne would find his issue in the indictments in December 1977 of twenty-four men accused of a variety of sexual offenses against adolescent males.[222] What followed was a campaign in a turbulent election year that would lead, among other things, to a determined, relentless and successful effort to destroy Robert Bonin's career in public service by forcing his removal as chief justice of the Massachusetts Superior Court. In 1978, Massachusetts politics would be torn asunder, a world gone mad.

PART THREE

The Devil in Massachusetts

CHAPTER 1

Wonderland

P EOPLE HAVE LONG BEEN drawn to Revere Beach, the
three-mile expanse of sand following the coast's gentle
curve just north of Boston. From the sky the beach appears
as an elegant crescent capturing and taming the waters of the
Atlantic—a stunning natural resource famed for its gentle surf
and cool ocean breezes.

Revere Beach was a prime recreational spot through most of
the nineteenth century. A poster from the 1880s describes the
beach as "the most beautiful sea shore resort in New England,"
featuring "music day and evening" as well as "electric lights
and fireworks."[223] There was a large measure of truth in this
advertising. The great Ocean Pier, projecting nearly two
thousand feet over the Atlantic, contained two great halls for
dancing by moonlight as well as a seven hundred and fifty foot
long roller skating rink. The Ocean Pier was a great success,
and a variety of hotels, cafes and recreational facilities soon

followed.[224] By 1895, sixty to seventy thousand daily visitors were pouring into Revere Beach.

The beach attracted the impressionist painter Maurice Prendergast, who likened it to the coast of southern France. Prendergast was so taken by the beauty of the place that he captured the pleasures of the Revere seaside in a series of watercolors painted during the summer of 1896. In one small painting, Prendergast depicts a tranquil scene of women with parasols and children frolicking in the blue water—a moment so quintessentially American that the piece was presented to Jacqueline Kennedy in 1962 for inclusion as part of the White House art collection.[225] But the idyllic image of the beach captured by Prendergast was not destined to last.

Over the years a collection of entrepreneurs and land speculators encouraged an explosion of amusements and other diversions at Revere Beach. The great natural resource of the beach served as a backdrop to a series of grandiose and tasteless commercial activities, most disagreeably in a monstrous amusement park developed by land speculators early in the twentieth century.

A Boston real estate broker, John J. Higgins, managed to acquire almost thirty acres of land just yards beyond the beach.

Higgins and his business partner, Floyd Thompson, dreamed of building a state of the art amusement park on this site, a park to rival New York's famed Coney Island. The men first discussed the idea in March 1905, and lost no time moving forward. A one million dollar investment, an enormous sum in those days, enabled Higgins and Thompson to open their amusement park on Memorial Day, 1906. Billed as a "matchless, mystic city by the sea," offering visitors a "cataclysmic triumph of twentieth century entertainments," the park was designed to draw people away from the beach and into a make-believe world. It was called Wonderland, and it was an immediate success.[226]

You could do almost anything in Wonderland. For ten cents admission, you could cruise in a Venetian lagoon, tour a Japanese village (complete with a "replica" of Mount Fuji, created from the earth excavated to build the lagoon), walk along a boardwalk, experience the thrill of a circus ring, attend the theatre, and wander into a functioning hospital where you could gawk at the special attraction of "infant incubators with living infants." The park included a man-made mountain complete with railway, a roller coaster, and a twice-daily event called "Fighting the Flames," where a cast of over three hundred actors recreated a "marvelously realistic and soul-stirring reproduction of the conflagration of a city block" for the pleasure of the thirty-five hundred people who would crowd the bleachers specially constructed for viewing the staged disaster.[227]

The only way you would know that you were near a three-mile beach was to take the park's most popular ride, the "Shoot-the-Chutes." Entering a gondola, you would be transported up to the top of the chute, and plunged quickly into the lagoon below. At the summit, for a few seconds before the plunge, you could catch a glimpse of the neglected beach.[228]

During its first year of operation, two million visitors came to Wonderland. This vast influx of people and the very nature of the park had an unalterable effect on the character and the perception of Revere Beach. It was, as one chronicler of Boston's North Shore put it, "a bedlam of the bizarre, a nightmare of the spectacular, and one of the great playgrounds of the world—a Jekyll-Hyde sort of beach."[229] Despite its state-of-the-art illusions, gimmicks and thriller rides, the park was a short-lived success.

As the novelty of Wonderland's amusements wore off, it became harder and harder to maintain sufficient revenues to stay profitable. When it closed in 1911, the amusement park left behind a vast, run down wasteland and a beach that had been abandoned by those who sought a peaceful seaside refuge. It was the beginning of a long and steady decline.

In the years following the Second World War, the shoreline fell prey to landowners who erected a dreary honky-tonk facade of cheap amusement houses, carnival rides, greasy spoons, and flop houses. The beach gradually became home to a variety of small time hoodlums, nostalgic die-hards, and the urban poor who could not afford to own an automobile but who could still get to the beach on public transportation. Given such a constituency, there was little incentive on the part of city planners and elected officials to invest money or energy on the beach infrastructure.

By the late 1970s it was a grim and grimy place. The great Cyclone roller coaster, some 3,600 feet of track soaring one hundred feet over the beach was a marvel of stomach-wrenching thrills when it was built in 1925, but by 1970, it was so badly deteriorated and unsafe that it was delivered up to the wrecking ball in 1974. By 1977, only two amusement rides remained on the beach, the so-called "Tilt-a-Wheel" and the "Bubble Bounce Rides."[230] A pavilion near the mid-point of the beach, where bands once played music to fill summer nights, stood as a symbol of the decay surrounding it. Like much of the beach infrastructure it had fallen into disrepair and was permeated by the stench of urine and the stains of rust bleeding from neglected iron posts into its cracked concrete.

As the beach attracted fewer and fewer people, it became a prime location for clandestine activities. During the summer months, a portion of the beach became notorious as a place that attracted men who sought the company of younger men who, for whatever reason—money, experimentation, genuine desire—responded to their affections. They would meet at the old pavilion and across the street at the bathhouse, where on a given summer evening there might be as many as fifteen or twenty cars lined up, as one observer noted, "each one driven by one man alone, sex taxis waiting for a fare."[231] This part of the beach was "crowded every summer day with boys," wrote *Village Voice* reporter Frank Rose in early 1978, teenagers who came "from all over the Boston area ... [to] sell themselves on the beach, outside the bars, and inside apartments..."[232]

One of those apartments was rented by Richard Peluso, a thirty-seven-year-old self-employed seller of novelty items who supplemented his income by establishing a boy-for-hire business out of his Revere home. Peluso made his apartment available to many young men who needed a place to crash, and for older men who sought a comfortable and discrete place to have sex. It was secret and safe until June 1977, when local police were drawn to Peluso's apartment by information they were given by a school bus driver who had been charged and convicted of having sex with minors.[233]

The raid of Peluso's apartment on June 16, 1977 provided the police with a treasure trove of incriminating evidence: Polaroid photographs and "home movies" of nude and semi-nude boys and adolescents, marijuana, pornography, and names and addresses of men who used his apartment to meet and have sex with younger males.[234] The photographs and movies enabled county law enforcement authorities to identify sixty-three men and adolescents, some of whom agreed to testify before a grand jury.

By December, that testimony and the evidence found at Peluso's apartment led to the indictment of twenty-four men by Suffolk County District Attorney Garrett Byrne. The indictments charged the men with a variety of offenses, including statutory rape, indecent assault and battery, and sodomy. Among the men indicted were a fifty-year-old child psychiatrist, a twenty-nine-year-old social worker, and two men associated with the exclusive Fessenden School for boys. The indictments were a page one story in the Boston press, a local scandal that drew national attention.

In the past, Garrett Byrne would have spoken with Superior Court Chief Justice Walter McLaughlin about which judges would be assigned to these cases. In 1977, however, McLaughlin was out of power, having reached the mandatory retirement age for judges. In his place sat a new chief justice—a young man whose brief career as Frank Bellotti's first assistant attorney general had gained him the confidence of Governor Dukakis as the person best equipped to be an agent for change who would impose court reform on a reluctant judiciary. Garrett Byrne could not walk in to Robert Bonin's office to have a quiet chat about judicial assignments. Bob Bonin simply would not hear of it.

CHAPTER 2

"The Smartest Guy I Ever Met."

F RANK BELLOTTI'S SELECTION of Bob Bonin as his first assistant was the crowning point in his effort to transform the attorney general's office into a modern, first-rate law firm. Bellotti took many symbolic steps, but in the selection of the team of lawyers who would lead his office, he was focused on attracting young, bright and energetic lawyers to shake things up. Bellotti established a selection committee of notable leaders in the Boston legal community, including Hale & Dorr attorney Earle Cooley and Boston University Law professor (and future SJC Chief Justice) Paul Liacos. The selection committee understood Bellotti's desire to depart from the norm in the selection of division chiefs and bureau heads. They were especially committed to finding a first assistant who would embody the reform spirit of the incoming administration.

Cooley and Liacos knew Bob Bonin, and inquired of his availability. It was as much a surprise to Bonin as it was to many others that he was even considered for the position of first assistant attorney general. Bonin, a self-described liberal who usually voted for Democrats, informed Cooley and Liacos that while he was interested in exploring opportunities with them, they should know that he had not supported Bellotti in the general election. Such an admission might have called the question against him, but it did not. Cooley and Liacos knew of Bonin's reputation and skill as a lawyer, and Bellotti was interested in changing the image of the office, so the movement toward Bonin continued.

Bonin was intrigued by the possibilities. "I thought it would be interesting to work on making the attorney general's office more professional than it had been in the past," he recalled. "My law practice was doing okay. I was not rich, but I was getting along, and I had recently separated from my first wife, and I was interested in [the post] because it was different, and maybe I was feeling a little stale in the private practice of law and saw it as a challenge."[235] His wife Angela remembered that he was "sick and tired of practicing law."[236] Although accepting the position would mean a cut in his salary, Bonin decided to do it. "It occurred to me that it might be a wise career move if I ever wanted to do anything else, possibly go on the bench, possibly get an appointment of some kind."[237]

Bonin was asked to meet Bellotti one afternoon at the YMCA, where the newly elected AG conducted his daily fitness regimen. The two men, who had not previously met, spoke about the role the first assistant would play in the new administration. Bonin insisted that he must have direct access to the new attorney general if he were to take the post.[238] Bellotti agreed, and although there would be further discussions around the terms of Bob Bonin's transition into the public sector, the choice was made. Bellotti thought that Bonin was "the smartest guy I ever met," and he relied heavily on the strong recommendation made by Cooley and Liacos.[239] Not counting his three years in the Judge Advocate General's Corps, it was Bob Bonin's first public sector job in twenty years as a lawyer.

Robert M. Bonin grew up in the 1930s in what was then Boston's Jewish ghetto, the Grove Hall section of Roxbury. Grove Hall was a community of immigrants, the kind of neighborhood that served as the first stop for many who came from Europe in the second great wave of immigration at the turn of the century. Many East European Jews settled there, including Bob's father William, a Russian immigrant who in 1913 left the family *shtetl*, a small town between Kiev and Odessa called Zaskiv, for a new life in America.

Young Bob Bonin's Boston, like Garrett Byrne's, was a small and insular place. Grove Hall was an island with strict boundaries—"an enclave surrounded by the Irish," as described by the author Theodore White in his memoir of growing up in that neighborhood. In this place, as in all of Boston's parochial neighborhoods, a young man or woman grew up an environment where traveling the equivalent of one city block could bring you into alien, hostile territory.

The Jews of Grove Hall and the Irish of Dorchester did not always live comfortably with one another, and prejudice and preconceptions ran deep.[240] A prominent chronicler of Boston's history notes that it was "understood that Jews did business in Irish neighborhoods but were not welcome to live there." Indeed, the "rules of the game, clearly understood by everyone," required that in "personal affairs ... [and] social arrangements, each group was expected to reside in its 'own place' and associate with its 'own kind.'"[241]

The jazz critic Nat Hentoff, several years older than Bob Bonin, grew up in the same neighborhood. In his memoir of those times, Hentoff recalled that returning to Grove Hall from a day at Boston Latin School was a difficult experience. "Some of the parochial school boys growlingly reminded us we were Jewish, and back in Roxbury, at night, it was still foolish to go out in the dark alone. Back home, it still made a big difference where, in the old country, your parents were from."[242] Recalling his youth in Grove Hall, Bonin could not recall being subject to any overt antagonism because he was Jewish, but he was always aware that Boston was not a place where people of his faith carried much influence.

Bob Bonin attended the William Lloyd Garrison grade school, and, following in the footsteps of Hentoff and White and many other young men of this time and place, was admitted to Boston Latin School. Admission by examination to Boston Latin, the nation's oldest public school, was a significant achievement for a young man of immigrant parents, and usually meant that a promising future lay ahead. Bonin did not have an exceptional record at Latin, but it was good enough upon graduation in 1948 for him to gain admission to Boston University's College of Business Administration. There he did excel. He found the work easy but boring, and decided to enter a combined program with the Law School. Bonin received a Bachelor's degree from the Business School in 1952, graduating magna cum laude. His strong intellect and aptitude for the law led to his selection as editor of the Boston

University Law Review, and he graduated first in his law class in 1954.

The next decade found Bob Bonin engaged in putting together the building blocks of his adult life. He married and had two children, attended George Washington University as a teaching assistant and successful candidate for an LLM degree, and joined the Army's Judge Advocate General's Corps, where he spent three years before returning to Boston and the practice of law. Bonin's early career as a lawyer appears by all accounts to have been successful but not extraordinary, in all events unremarkable. He built up a solid law practice and taught at Boston University Law School in order to supplement his income. He was not animated by politics or drawn to government, but he developed a reputation as a bright, reliable lawyer. Few people, Bob Bonin among them, would have predicted the path his life would take as he approached early middle age.

The regularity of Bob Bonin's life changed abruptly with three disruptive events that took place in 1973. His father William, preparing to leave Boston for Florida and a well-earned retirement, suffered a fatal stroke. Fred Bonin, Bob's older brother and only sibling, also died following a struggle with leukemia. And Bob Bonin's nineteen-year marriage was beginning to unravel, leading first to a separation and ultimately, in 1974, divorce. Any of these events, taken singularly, would unsettle most people. Coming as they did in the same twelve-month period, they appear to have had a profound effect on the forty-three-year-old lawyer. His life until then had been a study in normalcy. Suddenly, he was the sole adult male left in his family. And he was finding a new partner to share his life with.

Bob Bonin met his second wife Angela in 1974 when he was handling a divorce case for one of her friends. Angela was drawn to a man she perceived as being "a lot of fun. He had an outrageous sense of humor, and he was passionate about a lot of things in his life."[243] She was thirty-one when they met, a young woman who grew up in the South, with a troubled marriage and two children, a woman who described herself in those years as "idealistic and naive in capital letters."[244]

Bonin represented Angela during her divorce, and Angela remembers thinking that he "was very attractive and very smart. He was probably the smartest man I had ever had any kind of relationship with."[245] He was, she recalled, a "great challenge" to her. Angela would read newspapers and magazines voraciously in order to stay informed on current events: "God forbid he should catch me in something I didn't know."[246] They were married on August 24, 1975 at Kehillath Israel Temple in Brookline.

In an unusual expression of endearment, Angela referred to her husband by his last name. "Bob is a pretty ordinary person's name," she explained. "I mean it's an ordinary name: Bob, Bobby, Robert. And you've got to understand, I was so madly cross-eyed in love with this guy, I didn't think he was ordinary at all, so to call him 'Bob' just didn't get it."[247] Angela's habit embarrassed her new husband, who recalled: "It was especially unuseful during the high publicity years."[248]

In the midst of this time of extraordinary change and turmoil in his personal life, Bob Bonin was suddenly thrust into a very different period in his professional life. He rose to the occasion, performing ably as the new first assistant attorney general. Thomas Kiley, Bonin's successor as first assistant, would contend years later that Bonin "made Frank Bellotti look good."[249] Kiley attributed substantial credit for professionalizing the attorney general's office to Bonin's guiding hand. While Bellotti made news by opposing rising state automobile insurance rates and suing President Gerald Ford for imposing allegedly illegal oil import fees, Bonin went about the business of creating a professional public law office. Bellotti relied heavily on Bonin's legal acumen, but he relied even more on Bonin's ability to focus on rebuilding the office.

With Bellotti's approval, Bonin ushered in a new era at the attorney general's office. A code of conduct was written, a law library was built and a professional librarian hired, and resources formerly the exclusive privilege of private lawyers in large law firms—competent support staff, word processing, budgets to allow an attorney to take depositions and prepare a case fully—were made available. Seminars in a variety of subjects were offered to the mostly young assistant attorneys general and much emphasis was placed on the quality of writing and oral advocacy skills. Morale soared, and Bellotti's office was the subject of rave reviews in the press and the legal community.[250]

Bonin was highly visible in the office. He would frequently roam the corridors and look in on the work being performed by the young staff of lawyers he helped recruit. His contributions to strategic thinking in the development of major cases were highly regarded. Bonin was "a worker bee. He went into the courtroom and was active in the administration of cases as well as the office," recalled Tom Kiley. Kiley, whose own legal skills were formidable, viewed Bonin as a "skilled analyst [who] saw issues very well. He had very sound writing skills."[251]

Bonin was considered "a tough attorney and a tough administrator—the man who said 'no.'"[252] Known for his brusque office manner—Bonin once informed a law student intern that the young man's casual attire, sweater and slacks, would not do in a professional law office and insisted that the intern return that day wearing suit jacket and tie—he could also be charming, instructing the same intern at an office party on the proper way to open a bottle of champagne (twist the *bottle* while holding the *cork* steady).[253]

Bellotti and Bonin also ushered in another innovation: the requirement that all assistant attorneys general serve on a full-time basis, prohibited from having any private law practice. Each lawyer hired by the office was required to sign a certification to that effect, and to submit that certification to the first assistant's office. Bob Bonin himself was a notable exception to this rule. When he accepted Bellotti's offer for the first assistant's post, he mentioned that there was one particular case that he needed to keep with him, a complicated anti-trust matter that he was handling in federal court for a valued client, the Conboy Insurance Company.

Bonin had represented Conboy for several years, and acted as its outside general counsel. He was friendly with one of the owners of the company, Martin Kelley, and the two men and their wives frequently socialized with one another. Bonin believed that the complexity and importance of the case required him to keep it, and he frankly admitted that the additional income he would receive from Conboy as a result of keeping the case ($1,000.00 each month) would ease the transition he was making from his successful law practice to the modest fixed salary of a public servant.[254]

"I explained that that case had been pending for some years, and I had worked on it, it was in the federal court," recalled Bonin. "The [selection] committee knew of it as a condition and Frank Bellotti knew of it and approved it. He didn't do it in writing, as far as I recall. I didn't have any reason to think it would become a matter of controversy, but it was clear to him, me and the committee that I was going to work on that case."[255]

CHAPTER 3

The New Chief Justice

M ICHAEL DUKAKIS set a high standard as he considered who he would choose to replace Walter McLaughlin as Superior Court chief justice. The successful candidate would need to have a strong reputation for legal competence and administrative ability, while sharing Dukakis's commitment to court reform. First Assistant Attorney General Robert Bonin fit the bill in a fundamental way.[256] He was young, progressive, smart and independent of the established judiciary.

The governor's legal counsel, Dan Taylor, recalled that he had "heard nothing but good news about Bonin. He was ready, willing and able." Taylor had worked closely with Bonin on a number of matters, and respected the latter's legal ability. Taylor viewed the potential for a Bonin appointment as a "unique opportunity. If you didn't get a person who was really going to do it [implement court reform], it would all be for naught."[257]

Dukakis observed Bonin's performance as first assistant and "was very impressed." Dukakis recalled that Bonin "was obviously very smart, very hard working. He was clearly committed to change, reform and modernizing the court system."[258] Tom Kiley recalled that "Bob was picked precisely because he was an outsider and to bring the administrative skills [to the court] that were thought to be lacking."[259] After several conversations, and carrying the imprimatur of Bellotti's endorsement, Dukakis assured himself that Bob Bonin was the person best able to undertake the challenge. The decision was made.

Bonin served as first assistant attorney general from January 1975 until March 1977, when he was appointed chief justice of the Massachusetts Superior Court by Governor Michael Dukakis. It was only the third time in the Superior Court's one hundred and eighteen year history that its chief justice was not selected from among the ranks of the sitting associate judges.[260] Bonin had taken the post of first assistant attorney general with the hope that it would lead to bigger, better things, and now, just two years later, he was the governor's choice to lead the state's trial court system into a new reform minded era.

Dukakis's choice represented a bold move: the selection of this young, liberal lawyer with limited experience in public service may have seemed unorthodox, but the challenge ahead was large, and the governor wanted to select a person with strong legal skills who would also have no ties to the entrenched judicial establishment. Bonin's appointment was the foundation stone upon which Michael Dukakis planned to build an historic effort to reform the state's court system. Announcing the Bonin nomination on January 19, 1977, Dukakis said that those "who know Mr. Bonin admire his integrity, brilliant legal mind, rare leadership qualities, fair and even temperament and demonstrated capacity for administration."[261]

Bob Bonin did not pause to give the governor's offer a second thought, but Angela Bonin had her reservations. As she later expressed them: "Politics is invasive. If you are chief justice you can never walk away from it. We were newly married, had been married a couple of years, we were having a life, and I didn't want that to change."[262] Angela Bonin could not have imagined how much change was in store for her and her new husband.

Outgoing Chief Justice McLaughlin was furious that Dukakis would dare appoint someone from outside the court system who was publicly committed to implementing the Cox

Committee court reform recommendations. He launched a powerful and unprecedented public attack against Bonin's appointment. Characterizing the governor's selection of Bonin as a "grievous mistake" and "insult to the court," McLaughlin alleged that "the governor in one fell swoop has destroyed the morale of the court and has openly insulted each of the forty-five judges on the court."[263] Referring to Bonin as a "stranger," McLaughlin complained that it would take the nominee "at least two years to find out how the court operates."[264]

The old chief's views were rooted in a burning animosity toward Dukakis, one that had both personal and political overtones. The governor's refusal to reappoint his brother, Richard McLaughlin, as registrar of motor vehicles was personal.[265] The chief justice had called Dukakis to lobby for his brother's reappointment, but the new governor "thought that was inappropriate" and refused to accommodate McLaughlin. "I was in to clean house and certainly wasn't going to reappoint folks."[266] McLaughlin's world was being threatened by a reform governor: who or what would be next?

The Superior Court was a closed society of established customs and protocols where seniority was very important and, in many cases, where fathers reared their sons. McLaughlin's son, Walter Jr., was the prime force behind the city's largest and most popular Bar Review course, "SMH"—the intensive, ten-week course that nearly every third-year law student hoping to practice in Massachusetts enrolled in to prepare for the bar examination. The younger McLaughlin represented a variety of notable clients, including the City of Boston, and had no compunction about appearing in Suffolk Motion Session to plead a case for a client, where a portrait of his father, the chief justice of the Superior Court, hung directly above the presiding judge. It was common practice for judges, courthouse officials and political leaders to have children working in the DA's office, and while no rule or law prohibited this, it was viewed by some as unseemly and inappropriate.[267] Such was the way business was conducted in the Superior Court of Suffolk County, and the idea that this system was changing, that new leadership not beholden or responsive to the established traditions was now in place, did not sit well with many.

Respected *Boston Globe* columnist Robert Healy exposed the motives informing the antagonism toward Bonin's nomination. "The courthouse has become one of the state's last real sources of patronage," wrote Healy. "The Cox Commission report cuts into this. There would be centralized budgetary and personnel policies ... all this is threatening to the old guard at the courthouse. And Bonin has become the point man in this controversy."[268]

McLaughlin's reaction to the Bonin nomination was also a reflection of his strong belief that the only opportunity for advancement for a talented Superior Court judge was the prospect of promotion to the position of chief justice. "I had so many judges in my court who were so capable of being chief justice that I thought it was wrong for Dukakis to make it a political football and pick somebody from outside the court. And I said so at the time, and I affirm it now."[269] This view, while strongly held, ran contrary to the facts. Several Superior Court judges had found their way to the appeals court, and to the state's highest court. But McLaughlin held firmly to the belief that these judges "take the job at a financial sacrifice, there is only one area of promotion—chief justice." He noted that seven or eight judges were members of the exclusive American Association of Trial Lawyers, a distinction among members of the bar reserved for the best trial lawyers. "The only thing they had to look forward to was ... the honor of being chief justice of the court." This was rich coming from McLaughlin who himself had leap-frogged over other jurists

Figure 6: The New Chief Justice
Bob and Angela Bonin celebrate Bonin's confirmation as the new Superior
Court Chief Justice, while Attorney General Frank Bellotti puffs on a
celebratory cigar.

with greater seniority when he was named chief justice after serving a mere three years on the bench.

McLaughlin's rage drove him to increasingly intemperate remarks. He accused Dukakis of having chosen Bonin as the result of a "deal" with Bellotti in return for the attorney general's support of the court reform bill.[270] Bellotti came quickly and firmly to Bonin's defense. "If anyone is damaging the morale of the Superior Court judges," said the attorney general, "it is McLaughlin."[271] Bellotti dismissed McLaughlin's charge that he and Dukakis had cut a court reform deal over the Bonin appointment. Dukakis was simply "not that kind of man," said Bellotti.[272] Years later, Dukakis would dismiss the accusation with a laugh. "If there is one lesson I've learned," said the one-time presidential nominee, "is that you simply don't question people's motives."[273] Even *Boston Globe* columnist David Farrell, not known to be a friend of the governor's, felt compelled to remind his readers that Dukakis "has his faults, but they do not include wheeling and dealing."[274]

McLaughlin's harsh words provoked a loose coalition of leaders in the legal and political community to attempt to derail the nomination. Tom Burns, the trial lawyer who had been critical of the Cox Committee, resigned from his post as chair of the joint bar association committee on judicial recommendations as a protest against the Bonin nomination, which he described as "unsuitable." Burns was at least candid enough to link his opposition to Bonin to the Dukakis court reform initiative. "It is my certain belief," said Burns, "that the proposed candidate [Bonin] is a creature of, and must be committed to, the Cox report."[275]

After his nomination, Bonin called McLaughlin and asked for a meeting. The two men met, "and it was a cold and distant meeting. He did not welcome me," recalled Bonin. "I said to him, 'I understand your views [against me], but having received the nomination I'm going to take the job, and I came up here to speak to you as your prospective successor.' He did not wish me well or make nice."[276] Then the courthouse insiders weighed in, through *Boston Globe* courthouse reporter Joseph Harvey.

The *Boston Globe* was now the city's newspaper of record, having outlasted most of the significant competition. When the venerable *Boston Herald* proved no longer financially viable and merged with the tabloid *Record American,* the *Globe* found itself the city's only "serious" newspaper. Under the leadership of Editor Thomas Winship, the *Globe* made significant strides to improve its quality and vibrancy, but the paper had a schizophrenic aspect, nurturing young, aggressive reporters while sustaining a stable of older reporters with good connections and few scruples about letting opinion, or a personal agenda, creep into the news. J. Anthony Lucas, in his panoramic portrayal of the city in the 1970s, aptly described the *Globe* as an "obsessively political" news outlet that "consistently overvalued opinion and undervalued fact."[277]

Joe Harvey was the epitome of the *Globe's* old guard. Harvey had been the *Globe* court reporter since 1950, and it was said of him that he "knew the Suffolk County Courthouse inside and out—better than many of the judges there. When you wanted to know what was going on, Joe was the person you called."[278] Harvey did not make reporting for the *Globe* his sole profession. He maintained an active law practice during the years he served as the *Globe's* courthouse reporter, something that would appear to have been a conflict of interest. Moreover, Harvey's reporting over the years had made him, in the eyes of prominent criminal defense lawyer Harvey Silverglate, a "virtual adjunct to the district attorney's office."[279] Against the plain evidence of the Cox Committee findings, Harvey had previously reported that McLaughlin had "distinguished himself as a ... most successful court administrator."[280] Harvey now weighed in with a series of articles antagonistic to Bob Bonin.

Harvey disclosed that Bonin had provided incorrect information on a questionnaire filled out as part of the judicial nominating process. The inaccuracies related to Bonin's disclosure that he had been arrested as a sixteen-year-old for disturbing the peace, when in fact he was eighteen at the time. Bonin also failed to report several cases in which he sued former clients for the recovery of legal fees. These were minor indiscretions, but the *Globe* gave Harvey's story prominent "page one" play in its Sunday edition on February 20.[281] Harvey's reporting did not change the recommendation of the governor's Judicial Nominating Commission, and provoked Joseph Bartlett, the president of the Boston Bar Association, to characterize the effort to embarrass Bonin as a "witch hunt" and declare that "I don't even know Bonin, and I'm outraged by the *Globe's* conduct."[282]

The stakes were high.[283] One *Globe* columnist declared that "not in recent years has a nomination been so bitterly fought by the courthouse crowd."[284] Judge Dermot Meagher, whose father John was the senior associate justice in the Superior Court, recalled years later that the "perception was that all the others were insiders, and Bonin was an outsider coming as a reformer. So if he's coming as a reformer there must be something wrong with them. Who's he going to reform— right? That's not a very pleasant way to come in."[285]

WBZ Television and Radio broadcast an editorial by its highly respected editorial director, Harry Durning, that was highly supportive of the Bonin nomination, declaring that a "completely phony issue was raised about the fact the new chief is to come from outside the ranks of present Superior Court justices."[286] WBZ found that Bonin had "the will and the skill" to implement court reform improvements, and as such was "an excellent choice" whose nomination "should be quickly approved." The *Globe* editorial page took note of "Mr. Bonin's oversights," explaining that "it would have been better had Bonin dotted all the *i*'s and crossed all the *t*'s [because] there is a good deal of political-judicial jealousy involved in this highly important post and any mistakes on the record are likely to be taken advantage of by those who would rather see somebody else holding it." The *Globe* failed to endorse Bonin's nomination, but recognized his "good record as a professor of law, trial lawyer and first assistant attorney general."[287]

In the end, the anti-Bonin tactics were unsuccessful. Dukakis stuck by his nominee, viewing the flap over Bonin's youthful indiscretions as "kind of silly, so we pushed [the nomination] hard."[288] On the day of the hearing before the governor's Executive Council, Dukakis and Bellotti pulled out all the stops to assure Bonin's nomination. Bellotti himself appeared at the confirmation hearing, along with two other Superior Court judges and several district attorneys (but *not* Garrett Byrne) to support Bonin. Dukakis had also made it known that in his view, the "controversy of recent days [was] in essence a controversy over far-reaching court reform proposals."[289]

Bonin's nomination was approved on March 2, 1977 by the state's Executive Council with only one member in opposition, Herb Connolly, who may have been unable to resist opposing the hand-picked choice of his old political foe Bellotti.[290] The *Herald American's* award-winning photographer, Mike Andersen, captured the moment of victory with an iconic photograph of Bob and Angela Bonin locked in a kiss, while Frank Bellotti stood off to the side contentedly smoking a large cigar.[291] The next day the *Globe's* editor, Thomas Winship, sent a handwritten note to Bonin, "just to tell you how disturbed I was with the play and handling of your nomination by the *Globe.*" Winship had been out of town during the coverage, and declared that "The p.1 stories were not the *Globe* we all know."[292]

The brief, bitter episode was an ominous beginning for Bonin, who kept his silence and let the moment pass. The *Boston Herald American,* in an observation not lost on his enemies, noted that at age forty-five, Bonin "could hold the position of chief justice for the next twenty-five years."[293] Bob Bonin, soon to be one of the most powerful men in the Massachusetts court system, was in the words of the *Boston Globe* a "judicial unknown."[294] He would not remain so for long.

CHAPTER 4

The Outsider Inside

R OBERT BONIN WAS sworn in as the Commonwealth's eleventh Superior Court chief justice at a State House ceremony on March 8, 1977. That evening, a dinner party was given to honor the new chief justice, arranged and paid for by his former client, Conboy Insurance Company. The dinner was Martin Kelley's way of celebrating the achievement and good fortune of his friend. Bonin was mindful of the need to check whether Conboy's hosting of the dinner would pose any ethical problems. He assured himself that it did not. "I recall at one point before the dinner wondering whether there was anything that prohibited it, and I think looking at the canons of judicial ethics and seeing there was nothing there. And we had the dinner. There was no cash purse or gratuity involved."[295]

Bonin was perfectly correct in his interpretation of the rules, but he failed to assess the impression such a dinner might give to others. It was the beginning of a series of serious lapses in judgment that would come back to haunt the new chief justice.

Bonin took office as an outsider with no prior judicial experience, appointed by an increasingly unpopular governor to administer a controversial court reform package. Bellotti recalled walking down a State House corridor with Dukakis after Bonin was sworn in, and Dukakis saying: "I guess we showed those guys," meaning, said Bellotti, that the entrenched powers "got a Jewish chief justice. The courthouse was really Irish in those days. I was never really accepted up there. Bonin was an outsider—and a *Jewish* outsider."[296]

Bonin's religion was never overtly made an issue against him, but the resentment generated by this significant difference from the "norm" in Boston was a presence that never left Bonin's side. Harvey Silverglate recalled disparate treatment of Jewish lawyers at the bar by certain judges whose contempt "was visceral."[297] Bonin's outsider status—the fact that he had not come up through the judicial ranks, his alliance with the state's two great political outsiders, Dukakis and Bellotti, and the stark reality that he was appointed to implement the Cox Committee recommendations—was underscored (as if it needed underscoring) by his status as a man with a very different ethnic and religious background from the vast majority of men and women who populated and ran the legal and judicial systems in Boston. In the halls of the old courthouse in Pemberton Square, snide references to the "Jew-diciary" were sometimes heard among the whispers of the men who roamed the halls in search of clients and camaraderie.[298]

With the establishment stacked against him, Bonin needed to navigate the turbulent waters of courthouse and statehouse politics with some measure of skill, but he was ill-equipped to do so. "I didn't know much about Massachusetts politics, and Angela didn't know anything about it," Bonin recalled.[299] He was also politically isolated. The fact was that the new chief justice, as Bonin later admitted, "didn't know anyone. This is part of the problem as the case develops and progresses. The only important backer I had was Frank Bellotti. I was apolitical. I didn't have anyone to go to, to help me. It never really occurred to me."[300] Later, in the midst of their troubles, his wife Angela would recall a conversation she had with her husband when he was appointed chief justice. "I said to him, 'But isn't this a political job?' And he said, 'No, don't be silly, this is the judiciary.'"[301]

Bonin was gracious to his predecessor Walter McLaughlin, despite the note of asperity that had marked their first meeting, remarking to *Lawyer's Weekly* that "Justice McLaughlin did wonders considering present budget restraints."[302] Bonin made an effort to meet with each of the Superior Court judges, often at small dinner gatherings hosted by Angela at their home, in order to benefit from "their experience and wisdom" before adopting any of the Cox Committee recommendations. He also decided that despite the burden of his administrative responsibilities, he would sit on cases because he believed that "a chief justice has to sit to demonstrate to the other justices and to the public that he is capable of sitting and also to gain awareness of the problems facing the sitting justice."[303]

Bonin moved quickly to implement the court reform recommendations. A little over a month after taking office, he took a survey of the associate Superior Court judges and found to his surprise and delight that a majority supported "almost all" of the Cox Committee recommendations.[304] Bonin provided the results of his poll to the media, and lobbied for speedy legislative implementation of certain of the reform proposals. The poll gave the governor a chance to weigh in with the observation that the judicial system "doesn't work, is unaccountable and fragmented."[305] It seemed a fast and fine start to a career that, if left undisturbed, could last a quarter century.

District Attorney Garrett Byrne was one of Bonin's first

visitors. Byrne, recalled Bonin, "asked to meet with me and wanted to discuss the First Criminal—the assignment session—and the assignment of judges to particular cases such as what they called major offender cases. He wanted to talk about that and the assignment of cases and I told him I wouldn't do that unless defense counsel were present at the same time. I had been told that he would routinely meet with McLaughlin to decide the assignment of certain cases to certain judges."[306]

The *ex parte* discussions that took place between District Attorney Byrne and former Superior Court chief justice McLaughlin regarding judicial assignments were considered a significant abuse of power by members of the criminal defense bar. Harvey Silverglate, usually not at a loss for words on most subjects, exclaimed when asked about the practice: "I can't describe the atmosphere of trying civil liberties and civil rights cases in Boston in those days. We had to deal with these fascists."[307] McLaughlin and Byrne would "assign the cases they really wanted a conviction on to a small group of judges who didn't give a damn about defendants rights, and it was impossible to get fair trials from them."

In an article he wrote at the time, Silverglate expanded on this point:

While McLaughlin was chief justice, the district attorney's office all but took over certain aspects of the administration of the court. The most important of these was the scheduling of cases and the assignment to particular judges. Each morning scores of cases that appeared on the trial list for that day were assigned for trial or otherwise disposed of (postponed perhaps) by the judge sitting in the First Criminal, or assignment session. At the time the Superior Court had a large number of judges who had no respect for a defendant's rights or for the concept of fairness... A defendant who had his case assigned to one of the bad judges could expect not only a quick conviction, but a sentence at least two or three times as long as one that would be imposed by even a moderate judge... During the McLaughlin administration, Byrne's office had a great influence over such assignments. The judges in charge of the assignment session really did not know very much about what was going on—about what cases were to be tried, and which judges were free and which were occupied... Byrne had an assistant district attorney become a fixture in the assignment session and given the situation, it was easy for Byrne's representative to serve as a kind of secretariat for the court, recommending to the judge which other judges might be available to take which cases. In this way Byrne's office was often able to get the judges it wanted assigned to the cases it was most interested in.

Now, said Silverglate, Byrne and McLaughlin were still a "team" — this time, a team determined to remove Bonin from office.[308]

Bonin considered the judicial assignment practice inappropriate and unethical. "A district attorney should not be able to go to the chief judge and say, 'we have this serious murder case or some other kind of case and I want it assigned to Judge X.'"[309] Bonin believed that the district attorney could appropriately ask for a special assignment to a case, due to unique circumstances, but "when the request for a special assignment is made both sides should be present and have the right to say whether they agree, who they would like assigned, what they are looking for—it should not be done behind closed doors between the court and the district attorney." Bonin offered the district attorney that opportunity, but Byrne rejected it. "People told me that Byrne was pissed off, the feedback was that he was unnerved that he no longer had the access he had to Walter McLaughlin."[310] The two men met only rarely thereafter.

For those who traditionally held power in the revolving door of Boston politics what was clear was that power in the court house had now shifted to Bob Bonin. And that power was considerable. Bonin's handling of judicial assignments was no small matter. In the closed world of the trial court case assignments were a chief way to wield power. The person who made judicial assignments not only was able to accommodate favored judges who sought prized cases (or, in some cases, little work), he was able to influence a case by directing it to judges with proven predilections. As Silverglate put it, "For criminal defendants the assignment session became the whole ball game, the big lottery that determined their fates."[311]

When Walter McLaughlin was chief justice, he shared that authority with District Attorney Byrne, who used it to great effect. "Defendants who had not co-operated by pleading guilty and accused who were particularly unpopular with the district attorney's office would find themselves drawing the toughest judge for trial or sentencing," said Silverglate. "Even in very serious or capital cases, which by court rule were supposed to be assigned especially by the chief justice rather than by the assignment session judge, Byrne's office almost always was able to get assigned to one of his preferred judges."[312]

This potent power—a power that, when used, undermined the basic principles of fairness and impartiality that are the hallmark of the American judicial system—was taken back by Robert Bonin upon his arrival as chief justice. "Certain judges never moved," Bonin recalled. "Some favorites were getting to sit in better places than others, so there was some moving around of that which probably irritated some people. I did try very much to accommodate their wishes and keep people happy, but there were some changes."[313]

Bonin also demonstrated his new power over the judges who had previously experienced a hands-off attitude by the former chief justice. A case in point involved Judge Henry Chmielinski, who, according to Bonin, was "charging for lodging or some expense in connection with sitting somewhere, when he in fact had a summer home or home where he was sitting." These expenses involved what Bonin "considered to be an inappropriate charge to the Commonwealth on an expense report. I asked about it and was told 'he's been doing it for years.' I took it as an inappropriate charge, and I called Judge Chmielinski and I told him. He fussed and fumed and said he had been doing it for years, and that no one had ever questioned it before, and he resented it."[314] Bonin, who had no history and few personal relationships with the judges, could act as saw fit. He disallowed the expenses.

As one reporter put it, Bonin "took away several high-paying court-affiliated jobs that had traditionally been awarded on a 'buddy' basis. He cracked down on judges with padded expense accounts and made sure they worked full days and took no more than one month's vacation. He incurred the animosity of old guard judges and courthouse personnel who did not see him as a team player."[315] Bonin had, early on, been "charged, tried and convicted of being an outsider to the clubby legal and judicial establishment, for he is a symbol of and a catalyst for change."[316]

Curiously, Bonin made no changes in his own office. Although he hired three women who had worked for him at the attorney general's office, Bonin retained McLaughlin's staff, including the two office administrators, Francis X. Orfanello and his associate, Francis Masuret. "A couple of people mentioned to me that Orfanello didn't work very hard, and was very tight with Walter McLaughlin and that I could not be sure of his loyalty," recalled Bonin. "I kept my eyes open and gave him a chance."[317]

CHAPTER 5

Straw in the Wind

I F BOB BONIN represented a new day in the history of the court system, his wife Angela confirmed that the times really were changing. Young, outspoken on social issues, a stylish figure with striking blonde hair, Angela found herself frequently in the public eye. She was named "Boston's second sexiest woman" by *Boston Magazine* (second to Joan Kennedy and ahead of the actress Faye Dunaway), and her outspokenness led some to label her as "Boston's Martha Mitchell,"[318] the wife of Richard Nixon's attorney general who became briefly famous for her unorthodox public behavior. Angela was, in the words of one observer, "very bright, aggressive, ambitious, a driving force."[319]

Despite her public persona, Angela Bonin was a conventional woman, devoted to her husband and her children, fiercely loyal to them and protective of their interests. What made her unconventional in 1977 and 1978 was her reluctance to take a back seat to her husband when it came to public affairs and her frank, unvarnished way of speaking. It was, to be sure, uncommon for a wife of a Massachusetts judge to be a public figure in her own right. Angela was a described in the press as "glamorous but too ingenuous, and too earthy, to be chic."[320] Times were changing. Young, educated women were unwilling to recede into the background. If that young woman was both beautiful and the wife of a prominent figure, it was predictable that she would be the subject of fascination and scrutiny. Angela Bonin was good copy for a hungry local media.

Angela failed to ingratiate herself with the wives of Bonin's judicial colleagues. She would attend judicial conferences with her husband, and while he was busy with work and meetings she would go off alone, shunning events organized for spouses. Much younger than most of the other judicial wives, Angela was drawn to outdoor activities and would arrive at late afternoon cocktail parties still dressed in blue jeans and sneakers.

Angela remarked several years later that when her husband became chief justice, she "didn't get that I needed to re-draw myself."[321] At a conference in Sturbridge, Massachusetts in October 1977, a lunch was given to introduce her to the wives of some of the judges. One of the wives approached her and remarked, "Oh I'm so glad to see that you're appropriately dressed." Angela was "stunned because I didn't know that I had screwed up already. I didn't realize it. And they introduced me as 'Mrs. Chief Justice,' and I laughed, because I thought it was funny, but they were serious."[322]

Bonin's tenure on the bench was remarkable for its naiveté and contentiousness. He did not pay heed to the *Globe's* warning that "any mistakes ... are likely to be taken advantage of by those who would rather see somebody else holding" the post.[323] Perhaps one part of the problem was the sense that he had made it, he was holding an office which most people filled until mandatory retirement, and therefore was beyond the reach of those who would oppose him and court reform. Judge Dermot Meagher explained that "there is a certain euphoria after one is appointed. You kind of think you are untouchable. I would sit there and pinch myself and say 'what a great job this is.'"[324] Angela Bonin observed, "You know my husband missed a phase in his development. Most of us go through that idealistic stage where we want to save the world when we're in our twenties, but he didn't go through it until he was in his forties. When he became chief justice he had in his mind he was going to be there for twenty years and he was going to make a lot of changes."[325]

Bonin was criticized for imposing a lenient sentence on a young woman accused in a failed armed robbery attempt. Rita Landman was a Hampshire College student and the daughter of a prominent and wealthy New Jersey physician, and her sentence of two years probation was in stark contrast to the heavy jail sentences her two male accomplices received. What made matters worse was that Bonin was not the trial judge. He had taken the case way from Henry Chmielinski for sentencing purposes "and that was just unheard of that anyone would do that," recalled Dermot Meagher. "That's just not done."[326] Bonin left the impression that the privileged woman had received special treatment when, in fact, he had merely followed the prosecutor's recommendation. But the facts rarely matter in a case where emotions, not logic, rule the day. It was not a lesson Bonin learned easily.

Accepting the post of chief justice may have been an important professional opportunity, but it also meant another pay cut for Bob Bonin, and he was experiencing financial difficulties. After being sworn in he remarked in one interview that he might continue to teach a course in Evidence at Boston University Law School because "judicial salaries are so low I could use the extra money."[327] Angela Bonin recalled: "We were really living on very tight money. Bonin was paying alimony and child support, and then his middle son started college at Columbia."[328] Bob Bonin remembered that after he became chief justice he "was having a lot of financial difficulty in making ends meet, in paying alimony and child support, and trying to contribute substantially to the support of Angela and her two children."[329] There was also tension between Bob and Angela "about the disproportion in the amount I was paying out and what I had available for our family."[330]

One evening shortly after the chief justice took office Angela invited a group of friends including Martin Kelley to a dinner party. At dinner Angela mentioned that her car had been stolen. She was concerned this would harm her fledgling real estate business, which required her to be mobile. Kelley later, in conversation with Bonin, offered to buy a car for Angela. The then-existing judicial canons of ethics allowed such gifts to be made and accepted by a judge as long as "the donor is not a party or other person whose interests have come or are likely to come before him," and if the value of the gift is reported as outside income,[331] but Bonin declined the offer, believing "it was an imposition on our friendship. It was too grand."[332]

Kelley later offered to pay the monthly costs for a leased vehicle for Angela until she could get her business off the ground. Bonin met with Kelley and again informed his friend that he was "unhappy about the idea of presuming upon his friendship, and didn't wish to presume upon his friendship."[333] The decision was not his alone, however. "My wife was present. We agreed [to Kelley's offer]."[334]

There is no evidence—none was ever uncovered after months of investigation in 1977 and 1978—that Kelley's beneficence was due to anything other than his close personal friendship with and respect for Bob Bonin. But the absence of any direct conflicts or *quid pro quos* did not diminish the appearance that Kelley or his insurance company might enjoy favorable treatment from the chief justice if the occasion ever arose.

Governor Dukakis's chief legal counsel, Daniel Taylor, would later remark that Bonin's separation and divorce after nearly twenty years of marriage was "the straw in the wind" that should have been a signal that Bonin's judgment during that time might not be wholly reliable.[335] Taylor believed that Angela brought out a "lack of restraint" in Bonin—a tendency to recklessness that was unexpected coming from the otherwise reserved chief justice.

That recklessness was prominently on display in late 1977, when Bob Bonin was in court, not as a judge but as petitioner. Bonin sought a Probate Court reduction of alimony payments to his first wife, Phyllis, as his alimony and child support payments totaled almost twenty thousand dollars a year—nearly half of his thirty-nine thousand dollar salary as chief justice. During the course of the proceedings, Bonin made a full disclosure of his financial condition, including Angela's use of the leased vehicle—a 1977 Ford LTD—from Conboy Insurance. A reporter from a local weekly newspaper was present, and reported on the proceedings. Bonin's disclosure of the leased vehicle and his attempt to reduce his alimony payments quickly became front page news in the Boston papers, and created a firestorm of controversy and much fodder for his detractors.

Bonin's disclosure surprised his allies. Dukakis was particularly taken aback by the disclosure. He recalled:

> I remember one day I was taking the street car to work and it broke down at Kenmore Square. I found myself with a lot of other people walking down Commonwealth Avenue, and somebody who was an assistant clerk or something in the Superior Court introduced himself to me. I forget who he was. We were walking along and the guy said to me: "you know, I was very unhappy when you picked Bob Bonin." This is when Bonin has been in office three, four

months maybe. The assistant clerk said: "I just want tell you the guy's terrific, it's a pleasure working with him and he is really doing stuff and, you know, I'm excited and I just wanted to tell you I was wrong." And I'm feeling terrific, you know. Then about two days later I read about this alimony thing. Wow. Lord.[336]

When asked about the flap at a State House press conference, Dukakis said, "I can't direct the chief justice to do anything ... [but] I do think this arrangement should be terminated, the faster the better."[337] Bonin promptly terminated the lease. On November 30, 1977, he wrote to Allan Rodgers, the chairman of the Committee on Judicial Responsibility, that the lease "represents a gift each month by friends and former clients. None of the individuals or corporations associated with the gift have any litigation or business pending before the Superior Court." Nevertheless, and "despite there being no impropriety involved, because of the adverse publicity my wife and I have this day advised Conboy Insurance Agency to no longer make the lease payments on the automobile she uses."[338]

Bonin's action did not quell the political uproar. All of Bonin's old adversaries now emerged, each calling for his suspension or resignation. Tom Burns, who had resigned as chairman of the Bar Association's Committee on Judicial Nominations in protest of Bonin's appointment, called on the chief justice to resign, declaring that Bonin has "besmirched his own position, the judicial system as a whole and the cause of court reform."[339] Councilor Herb Connolly charged that Bonin had failed to resign as an officer of two corporations before assuming office as chief justice. The charge, if true, was a serious breach, but the State Secretary investigated it on an expedited basis and demonstrated the charge to be false.[340]

Connolly would not be deterred, and he orchestrated a 5-0 vote of "no confidence" by the Executive Council, demanding the judge's suspension pending further investigation of the lease.[341] Two Republican legislators also took up the cause, filing resolutions in the House and Senate seeking Bonin's suspension from office. The Supreme Judicial Court's Committee on Judicial Responsibility convened in order to determine whether and when further investigation of the chief justice would commence.[342]

The furor over Bonin's conduct began to undermine the court reform effort that he and Dukakis cared so deeply about. The *Globe,* in an editorial on December 6, asked the pertinent question: "Has Judge Bonin, by his actions, lost the confidence of his colleagues in the judicial system and abdicated his authority to lead one of the major divisions in what, we hope, will soon be a 'reformed' system of courts in the Commonwealth?"[343] An unnamed legislative leader and supporter of court reform worried that Bonin had "poisoned the atmosphere of court reform."[344]

The headlines were persistent and ominous in tone: the *Herald,* December 2: "Bonin's woes mount"; the *Globe,* December 3: "Impeachment material ready"; the *Herald,* December 4: "Lawyer to Bonin: quit"; the *Herald,* December 7: "Senator demands Bonin step down"; and perhaps the most startling in the *Globe,* page 1 on December 8: "Bellotti reportedly asks Bonin to quit." Dan Taylor, leaving government to regenerate his law practice at Hill & Barlow, watched helplessly as "the chance of a lifetime was going up in smoke."[345]

On December 7, the *Globe's* Pulitzer Prize winning editorial cartoonist, Paul Szep, featured the embattled chief justice holding up a card reading simply: "I am not a sleaz [sic]." Bonin was bleeding badly. He maintained a strict public silence, but Angela told a *Globe* reporter: "My husband is not going to resign. And you can take your fifteen *Globe* reporters that you've assigned full-time on my husband and just keep it up. But you are not going to pressure us into anything. My husband has not done anything wrong. I don't know what is behind this effort by the *Globe* but let me assure you that if you expect my husband to resign, you are in for a long siege."[346]

Angela's very public role in her husband's defense was uncommon for a political wife in 1977. Bob Bonin described himself as "a woman's rightist, and my wife makes her own decisions." This was confirmed by Angela, who made it clear that "I don't ask my husband for permission to make statements because we don't have that kind of relationship."[347] In fact, Angela was savvier than her husband about the need to deal effectively with the press. As she later explained: "We had no experience being in big public politics. I was visible when my husband was being attacked because he had no spokesperson, he had no one to defend him. If the media or just an individual puts forth one point of view then that will be the perception until that point of view is somehow balanced or countered, and there was no way to do that. And I kept my mouth shut for a very long time."[348]

The Legislature rejected a Republican move to suspend the chief justice by failing to come up with the two-thirds vote necessary to suspend its rules and take up the motion, but ominously for Bonin a substantial majority (138 to 79) voted for the rules suspension.[349] The reprieve in the Legislature, and the proximity of the winter holidays, all appear to have calmed the furor. But the episode had damaging political consequences for Bonin that would leave him without significant allies in the future.

Dukakis viewed the controversy with some concern. "First it was the petition for reduction of alimony. It just struck me as being very poor judgment. He shouldn't have taken the job if he thought he was going to have to do that." But it was the leased car that really rankled. "That was more bad judgment in my opinion. I mean, you're a judge now, you don't accept gratuities from anybody. I was beginning to say to myself 'Jeepers, Bob is a very bright guy, an able guy, what's going on here?' We all exercise bad judgment from time to time. But you get a series of these things in that kind of position, you really have to say to yourself something's wrong here."[350]

Globe columnist Robert Turner opined that the flap had damaged both Dukakis and Bellotti: "For Bellotti the problem is a dual one, of credibility and performance ... for Dukakis, the problem is one of judgment." Bonin's actions "constitute a pattern of conduct on the edge of judicial propriety," wrote Turner, noting that Dukakis "was visibly disappointed with his appointee, and a number of people, many of whom had questioned Bonin's qualifications all along, were disappointed with Dukakis."[351] *Globe* columnist David Farrell, who was known to have close ties to Bellotti,[352] warned that Bonin was "likely to have greater worries if he doesn't put an end to the expanding probe" by stepping down.[353] Bonin, said Farrell, was left "with no cards to play." Ominously, the Committee on Judicial Responsibility asked prominent attorney Robert Meserve to commence an investigation into the matter.

But Bob Bonin would not step down. He believed that he had complied with the letter of the law, and that the storm would fade. He sensed that once a full review of the matter was completed, he might be slapped on the wrist with a mild rebuke, but no more. Bonin himself moved quickly to put the incident behind him. He had already put an end to the automobile lease. Now it was time to put the alimony controversy to rest. On December 29, 1977, he asked the Probate Court to dismiss his petition for alimony reduction, a request that was promptly granted.

Meserve's report found that the charges against Bonin were

either unproven or unworthy of disciplinary action.[354] The incident regarding the leased car was harmful, but not fatal to the chief justice. His enemies knew this as well as anyone. They would have to be content with simply embarrassing the chief justice for now, unless Bonin would accommodate them and provide them with additional ammunition.

It was time for Bob Bonin to return to the business of administering the trial court system. The Superior Court docket was clogged, the system understaffed and in need of reform. Many significant cases awaited trial, not the least of which were cases arising from Garrett Byrne's indictments of twenty-four men accused in the so-called "Revere sex ring." There was much to do.

CHAPTER 6

An Act of Revolution

O N DECEMBER 8, 1977, as the Boston press was maintaining daily coverage of the chief justice's woes, another story appeared on the front pages: the indictment in Suffolk County of twenty-four men in a "sex ring" that involved sex with minor and adolescent boys. The men, some of whom were shown being led into court for arraignment, were identified by name and address in both daily papers. Among them were a prominent Boston child psychiatrist and two men associated with the highly respected Fessenden School for boys.[355] All were charged with various counts of assault and battery, sodomy and statutory rape.[356]

The average age of the adolescents named as victims in the indictments was fourteen.[357] Despite the obvious impropriety, there were indications that many of the boys did not find the sexual advances unwelcome, and were perhaps complicitous in the conduct. It was an open secret that many boys—boys who were seeking money, companionship or sex with older men—frequented Revere Beach and a particular house on Mountain Avenue in Revere.[358] Yet at least a few of the boys, after some encouragement from law enforcement officials, were apparently prepared to testify in court in support of the DA's case.[359] One seventeen-year-old told the *Globe,* "No matter how much I try to block that part of my life out, the scars will never go away."[360]

The district attorney's office did not mince words or actions when it came to describing the nature of the alleged crimes. "This is a bunch of guys who liked to get together and party with little boys," exclaimed Assistant District Attorney Thomas Peisch. "This is sex for hire."[361] District Attorney Byrne called a press conference and vowed to push forward with an investigation of the "Revere sex ring," declaring, without evidence, that these indictments were merely the "tip of the iceberg" and warning of more arrests to come.

Byrne established a hotline, and urged citizens who knew or suspected anyone of having homosexual contact with minors to call anonymously and turn in their evidence or suspicions.[362] Even State Representative Elaine Noble, the state's first openly homosexual elected official, supported the hotline, urging constituents and others to call in because she believed that adults "involved in the corruption of unprotected, impressionable children by drugs, alcohol and sex must be immediately halted and reprimanded." Noble called a press conference to denounce the "gross personal abuse and affrontery on innocent children," which she termed "a sacrilege of the highest order."[363]

The hotline was the instant success feared by many. During one forty-minute period, the district attorney's office logged twenty-five telephone calls to the hotline.[364] After the first full day in operation the hotline had received one hundred calls from anonymous persons who wished, in Byrne's words, to "provide more information about the present case and about similar crimes."[365] Byrne's hotline created a furor among civil libertarians and the increasingly vocal and confrontational gay community in Boston. Explaining the dangers of the "hotline" concept, Harvey Silverglate noted that hotlines by their nature create hysteria by encouraging all sorts of people with all sorts of agendas to make anonymous charges. "It singles out an area in which you are saying: 'you give us uncorroborated evidence because we deem these cases to be of higher importance than others.' The subliminal message is that the prosecutors will move forward with slim evidence."[366]

Hotlines help undermine the fundamental premise that an accused should be confronted by his or her accusers, and encourage an approach where the focus is not on the crime but on the person, making law enforcement officials focus on finding facts to satisfy the claims against the individual. Silverglate paraphrased Alan Dershowitz, observing that hotlines help law enforcement officials to teach their witnesses not just to sing, but also compose. Opposition to the hotline drew support from a broad spectrum of citizens and civic leaders who believed that Byrne had gone too far, and that the use of a telephone hotline to receive unevaluated and anonymous accusations was both poor law enforcement practice, and a threat to the reputations of innocent people.

But the district attorney would not back down. Byrne had just received the news that his first assistant, Newman Flanagan, was leaving the office in order to consider whether he would challenge Byrne for re-election the following year. Byrne probably saw the hotline as that rare combination of good law enforcement and good politics, and he was determined to stay the course, but he profoundly misunderstood the tenor of the times. Significant public opposition to the hotline was unthinkable in Garrett Byrne's Boston—the Boston of the Watch and Ward Society, the Boston of the 1930s, a time when the city's mayor exercised his municipal powers to prevent Lillian Hellman's play *The Children's Hour* from performing in Boston, because he found the play's sympathetic portrayal of a lesbian "so revolting that I think the people of Boston do not need to see the show."[367]

In Garrett Byrne's heavily Catholic, buttoned-down Boston, attitudes toward homosexuality were predictably hostile. There was no greater evidence of this than the disastrous end of the long career of David Ignatius Walsh. Walsh was a prominent figure in Massachusetts politics during the first half of the twentieth century, serving as the Commonwealth's first Irish Catholic governor and for several terms as United States Senator. He grew up in the rural central Massachusetts town of Clinton—a small town boy with big city ambitions who offered a stark contrast to the rogues and wise guys of the big city.[368] Devout in his religious beliefs, Walsh was also a lifelong bachelor, long rumored to be homosexual.[369]

In 1942, as the nation was in full war throttle, the *New York Post* reported on a Nazi "spy nest" operating out of a male brothel in Brooklyn. The newspaper identified Walsh as a frequent visitor to the brothel, causing a furor in Washington. Walsh was chairman of the Naval Affairs Committee, and potentially a significant security risk if indeed he frequented the place. He denied the story as a "diabolical lie," and the Washington establishment, led by the FBI who persuaded a key witness to change his prior testimony about Walsh, came strongly to his defense. But the damage had been done. Walsh suffered a crushing defeat at the polls in 1946, losing to Henry Cabot Lodge, Jr. by nearly four hundred thousand votes, and he died the following year a broken man.[370]

If indeed Walsh was gay (and the evidence points in that direction), the idea that he would be a visitor to a male brothel is not surprising, given the utter lack of opportunity in those days for gay men and women to meet others of the same orientation in more open settings. In a society that frowned upon any public acknowledgment that same-sex attraction even existed, it was impossible for gay men and lesbians to enjoy an open social life. This was, after all, a society that regarded same-sex attraction as an illness or perversion, whose federal government made the mere fact of homosexuality grounds for a mandatory dismissal from a government job.[371] The closets that most gay men and lesbians inhabited during most of the first half of the twentieth century were dark and tightly closed.

Boston in 1978 was a changed place. The great civil rights movement of the 1950s and 1960s and the influence of the many colleges and universities in and around Boston had a liberalizing effect upon the city, and especially its younger residents. Elaine Noble won election to the state Legislature as an openly lesbian activist, and Boston Mayor Kevin White appointed a liaison to the gay and lesbian community, a young Irish Catholic activist, Robin McCormack.

Boston's gays and lesbians were a diverse group, and public figures like Noble and McCormack did not speak for all. Like the Irish before them, the political leadership of the gay community was divided along a deep fault line: those assimilationists who sought to become a part of and to work within the system, and activists of different stripes and with different agendas who rejected blending into the status quo. A great divide emerged between those who sought social acceptance and integration into the norm, and those who thrived on their status as outsiders and social renegades. Among those gay men who took a militant attitude and unconventional approach to gay liberation—who bridled at the suggestion that in order to "obtain any kind of acceptance we must show the middle-class that we pose no threat to them"—were members of the staff of a Boston publication provocatively entitled *Fag Rag*.[372]

First published in 1971, *Fag Rag* espoused a decidedly radical credo. The men of *Fag Rag* saw themselves as living "under a reign of sexual terror: wherever we move, we might be killed, beaten, abused ... our lives are worth little in the straight world."[373] To that end, they engaged in a robust culture war, opposing integration into the existing "patriarchal and capitalistic institutions," and rejecting the usual polite norms of political discourse.[374] Decrying the "deathtrap of respectability," their credo was plainly put: "We shit on propriety and we defy all images and appearances appropriate to and supportive of the straight society."[375]

Twenty-three years after its publication, a historian opined that *Fag Rag* "is of singular importance because it articulated a far more radical and isolationist view than the earnest coalition-building so common in gay politics."[376] One of the founders of *Fag Rag*, the Harvard-educated poet Charles Shively, described the newspaper's mission as helping to free an oppressed society by embracing the sexual act (in all of its potential forms) as an "act of revolution."[377] In a column entitled "Pure Sex," Shively called for "Self-indulgence, living our lives for ourselves, following our own desires, passions, feelings." He asked: "Isn't this what our liberation should be about?"[378]

The men of *Fag Rag* held particular disdain for other homosexuals who worked within established political power systems. They were savvy enough to know that "language itself is a revolutionary battleground," and used language to shock and provoke.[379] "Now is the time," wrote *Fag Rag* writer John Mitzel, when "we will either successfully create the intellectual revolution against the structures of current agencies of social control, or we fail. To succeed, we must ridicule, shut down, and discredit the new variety of apologists for the given order of things—i.e., the homo-ward healers in our midst."[380] The "accommodationist faction within our ranks," the "homo ward-healers" were defined by Mitzel "by their most striking characteristic: they are all absolutely obsessed with the *image* we project to the straight world."[381] Mitzel was left undaunted by the relatively small number of men who shared his views. He would say in later years, "A lot of change can be effected by a small group of people. There's always confluence."[382]

The perception of homosexuals as targets for abuse by mainstream society led to a call to intellectual arms: "it is time that the gay liberation remnant take up a new strategy, enter a new stage in the struggle," a strategy that required its proponents to "remain radicals, revolutionaries, sexual guerrillas, [and] outlaws…"[383] These men took their self-described roles as sexual outlaws seriously. Rejecting all conventional views—straight and gay—about sexual expression, they openly and enthusiastically advocated perhaps the most controversial and divisive conduct: sexual relations with adolescents. They opposed as archaic and puritanical the Massachusetts law that made sex with any person under age sixteen statutory rape, and believed that "intergenerational sex is going to be the movement's next big issue."[384] Their language was unapologetic and frank: "*Fag Rag* has been the most consistent voice in the tiny group taking on police, DAs, psychiatrists who are busy rounding up boy-lovers. The Kiddie Porn Panic of 1977 and 1978 has given an unchallenged license for the state to hunt down the pedophiles … who have an intense and affectionate interest in children."[385]

Central to this theme was a former Methodist minister and political activist who had come to Boston in 1972. Born in rural Tennessee in 1938, Tom Reeves combined a strong intellect with an equally strong Protestant faith to seek out a career in the ministry. His political radicalism and sexual orientation put him at odds with church hierarchy and soon compelled him to a different course. During most of the 1960s Reeves was the epitome of the restless, lost soul, moving from Alabama to Boston to Berlin to Washington and, finally to Baltimore, pursuing but not completing two doctorate programs and seeking work that would satisfy his activist tendencies. In 1970 he became a leader in the movement to end the draft, joined the American Friends Service Committee, and co-authored a book (*The End of the Draft: The Feasibility of Freedom*) with the prominent libertarian activist Karl Hess. Reeves offered his speechwriting services to several political leaders, and eventually found himself caught up in the effort to elect George McGovern president in 1972. It was during the 1972 Democratic National Convention in Miami that Reeves experienced a deep emotional crisis. He found himself sitting on the beach, engulfed by tears, unable to cope with the "terrific sense of not being myself, of not being a whole person." In short order he left Miami, returned to Baltimore, and came out to his colleagues at the American Friends Service Committee. When that did not go as well as he had hoped, he left Baltimore and hitch-hiked to Boston in the company of a young hustler. "Boston represented in my mind a place where

Figure 7: The Boston/Boise Committee
John Mitzel (l) confers with Thomas Reeves.

there was a lot happening around the gay struggle ... so that's where I came to find a new life."[386]

Boston would end up being the last stop for this restless activist: he found in the city a place where he could disentangle the cords that had bound him to an unfulfilled emotional life, and give voice to the strong sexual impulses and unorthodox opinions he had repressed and hidden for so long. Reeves was candid, consistent, and often dramatic in his approach to gay rights. John Mitzel, long a friend, sighed that Reeves "loves being the center of the brouhaha. Which of course can lead to trouble because, you know, sometimes you over-act your role. And I've seen that on numerous occasions."[387]

Reeves was unapologetically attracted to adolescent boys, and described himself as a pederast. He was quick to distinguish pederasty from pedophilia—in an interview in 1999, while embracing his attraction to post-pubescent male adolescents, he stated clearly "I am not a pedophile." He held firmly to the view that "within homosexual traditions in the world, pederasty is probably the majority tradition." His attraction to post-pubescent adolescent males was not a part of his overall sexual and political radicalism—it was a deeply rooted orientation. When challenged to admit that his views toward pederasty were decidedly minority opinions, Reeves exploded: "I'm sorry, it's a god-damned lie! I do not agree that it is a minority form or a marginal form [of sexuality]. Certainly it's the most controversial because that's where straight America has made its stand."[388]

As he wrote for *Fag Rag,* Reeves believed that it was still an open question that "we couldn't enlarge the definition of homosexuality to include pederasty." In a long essay published in 1978, Reeves referred to his coming to terms with his identity as a "boy-lover" as his second coming out. Alarmed that the "momentum of slander, censorship and imprisonment for sex between men and boys is growing," Reeves sought to portray these relationships as "quiet, enduring, reciprocal and certainly voluntary."[389]

Reeves made his case without qualm. Sex between men and boys "is certainly not pedophilia and absolutely remote to child molestation," wrote Reeves. It was "often a form of mutual learning and teaching." Moreover, Reeves sought to dispel the notion that intergenerational sex was inappropriate coercion. "Seduction of men *by* boys is at least as frequent as seduction *of* boys by men," he wrote.[390] John Mitzel, drawn to the struggle because of his "wish to dismember the structure of present-day oppressions," wrote that "The case of homosexual boy-lovers is the most clear cut of any on the political horizon today. As Tom Reeves has pointed out, man-boy love is usually an act of mutual rebellion against the tyranny of heterosexual norms being pressed in on them from all sides."[391] When District Attorney Byrne handed down his indictments it struck at the heart of what these radical gays were advocating.[392]

On December 9, 1977, *Fag Rag* staff members met around Tom Reeves kitchen table and formed the Boston/Boise Committee.[393] "We smelled lynching in the wind," wrote Mitzel. "[We] met and decided to do something."[394] The committee's name was an allusion to the trials in the mid-1950s of several homosexual men in Boise, Idaho. In his 1965 book, *The Boys of Boise, Time Magazine* editor John Gerassi wrote an account of what he described as a witch hunt against homosexual men. The Boston activists saw many similarities between the Boise scandal and what was happening in their city. Gerassi's account demonstrated that many of the boys from Boise who were alleged to be victims of homosexual advances were actually young toughs and hustlers who were taking advantage of their sexual partners for money.[395] This was also the opinion of the *Fag Rag* contingent: the boys who were having sex in Revere were not victims but willing participants, either street toughs willing to "be serviced" by older men who would pay for the opportunity, or gay youth looking for aid, comfort and direction.[396]

The committee had two primary goals: putting an end to the district attorney's hotline, and working to ensure that the men who had been indicted would received fair treatment in the midst of what was perceived as a public anti-gay panic being encouraged by Byrne.[397] Mitzel described the committee as "a civil rights group concerned with the civil rights of all homosexuals as a class of citizens during this homophobic witch hunt."[398] Mitzel stressed that the committee "from the start deliberately chose not to be a defense committee for any or all of the twenty-four men under indictment."[399] In this he was corroborated by Reeves, who recalled that Boston/Boise was "never a defense committee. We didn't try to function as a defense committee and raise money that went to the lawyers and the defense of any individuals."[400] This would be a large matter of contention later in 1978, when the purposes of the committee came under close public scrutiny, and Reeves, carried away by his own rhetoric, publicly referred to the group's work as providing funds for the legal defense team.

The Boston/Boise Committee represented a minority point of view in Boston's gay and lesbian community. State Representative Elaine Noble was vocal about her opposition to sex with minors. "Street kids are in a particularly vulnerable position," Noble said. "What they need is some guidance and support. The last thing they need is an adult father figure coming on sexually to them."[401] Many in the gay and lesbian community took their lead from Noble and decided to keep their political distance from the radicals. John Mitzel, one the leaders of the committee, chastised those who he sarcastically referred to as the "Good Gays,"[402] and nearly twenty years later he still had nothing but scorn for Noble. Reeves himself expressed "nothing but disgust" for Noble.[403] These views were shared by others. A quarter of a century later, passers-by could still see carved in a sidewalk on Boylston Street the words "Scut Noble."

Fag Rag published an "Emergency Supplement" asking: "Are You Next?" and attacking those "middle class elements within the gay movement [who] have consciously decided to pursue their own good at the expense of the more vulnerable: children, prostitutes, the promiscuous, working class and other especially mistreated homosexuals." "The idea," cried *Fag Rag*, "is to sacrifice the most vulnerable among us in exchange for acceptance from the Straight Community."[404] "There was," wrote John Mitzel, "panic in the gay community. Who was being secretly denounced to the police? Who would be arrested next and humiliated on the front pages of the press? No one knew. Not one voice was raised challenging the allegations of the police and the district attorney."[405]

The leaders of the Boston/Boise Committee were intelligent, energetic people who understood the power of the printed word and the ability to change public opinion through sustained organized efforts. The arrests and indictments coming out of the district attorney's office presented Reeves, Mitzel and their committee with an opportunity to employ their revolutionary rhetoric to challenge specific official conduct. The focus of their efforts was the eighty-year-old district attorney, Garrett Byrne.

On a cold, blustery mid-December afternoon approximately thirty activists took the then extraordinary step of demonstrating against the arrests and the hotline by picketing in front of Boston City Hall. In what was described by one journalist as "America's smallest gay rights demonstration of 1977," the activists held placards proclaiming "Dump the DA," "Stop Media Slurs" and "Defend the Rights of Boys and Men," and circulated a flyer that accused the press of publishing lies and attempted to make the best case for the Revere defendants: the sex was consensual, most of the boys were older adolescents.[406] Later, in April of the following year, they would bring the aging beat poet Allen Ginsberg to town, reading from a version of his poem *Howl* that had been revised especially for the occasion to include the lines:

> … [men] who were arrested for teenage porn ring headlines in the *Boston Globe*
>> when the octogenarian bachelor DA got hysterical screaming through his iron mask at election time
>>> lusting lusting lusting for votes, for heterosexual ballot boxes' votes …[407]

It was not in Garrett Byrne's interests to empower such a fringe group, but the district attorney did just that when he initiated the hotline. But Byrne, steeped in a moral tradition that was rooted in the first quarter of the century, had no personal frame of reference to help him understand the gay and lesbian community of Boston in the late 1970s, much less the political and sexual radicalism of the Boston/Boise Committee.

Many very different issues and causes—equal rights for gays and lesbians, consensual sex and the proper age of consent, contests for political power among the city's emerging gay and lesbian leadership—came together and blurred in the public perception. The Boston/Boise Committee viewed the hotline as an illegal and unacceptable threat to their community; many others viewed the hotline as a threat to civil liberties. The DA and his team were intent on holding fast to the indictments. The Boston/Boise Committee was determined to do something about it. Its members were on a collision course with Garrett Byrne, and Bob Bonin would find himself caught in the undertow.

CHAPTER 7

Beginning of the End: Eight Days in April

T HE BOSTON/BOISE Committee first did battle with the district attorney over the constitutionality of the hotline. The committee hired attorney John Ward to bring an action against Byrne, alleging that the hotline violated basic civil liberties of homosexual men. On December 28, 1977, at a hearing on the committee's request for an injunction halting the hotline, Byrne's office announced that it was voluntarily putting the controversial practice to an end.[408] Buoyed by this victory, the committee pushed forward with its demand that any information gathered as a result of the hotline be destroyed.[409]

The committee was also determined to find ways of providing assistance to the twenty-four men indicted in the Revere cases. On February 16, 1978, the committee's co-chair, Thomas Reeves, wrote a letter to each of the lawyers representing the Revere defendants, informing them that the committee had formed a media task force "that we hope will result in more sensitive treatment of the present cases," and an educational forum "on the issues raised by the present cases."[410] Reeves noted that the committee intended "to press the district attorney's office for assurances that the witch hunt aspects that the prosecution has assumed will be dropped in favor of a more temperate approach."

Reeves and other committee members met with several of the lawyers representing the defendants. They discussed the possibility of providing financial support to bring in the National Jury Project, an organization that provided assistance in the selection of unbiased juries in cases that had received inordinate and possibly prejudicial media attention. The Jury Project was an entrepreneurial outgrowth of the 1970s anti-war movement. In 1971, the federal government put several anti-war advocates, including the Catholic priest Philip Berrigan, on trial for a variety of alleged plots against the government and its selective service system. The trial was conducted in Harrisburg, Pennsylvania, the state's politically conservative capital. Sociologist Jay Schulman, himself an anti-war activist, determined to establish a level playing field for the defendants by volunteering his efforts. Schulman and a group of volunteers conducted a survey of the Harrisburg area, including in-depth interviews with two hundred and fifty-two citizens representing a sample of the potential jury pool.

Schulman provided defense counsel with a profile of an "ideal" juror: in this case, a female Democrat with no religious preference and a white collar job. Potentially "bad" jurors for the defense were, surprisingly, college-educated citizens, especially those with Protestant religious affiliation. These guidelines were used by defense counsel during the jury selection process. The verdict, a hung jury split 10-2 in favor of acquittal, appeared to be a stunning testament to the efficacy of scientific jury selection. Schulman went on to form the National Jury Project in 1975, and offered his services to counsel litigating difficult cases.[411]

Certain of the lawyers representing the defendants believed that the Jury Project would be of enormous assistance to them at trial. Defense Attorney William Homans believed that the Project "would be immensely helpful to us in having proper and meaningful *voir dire* questions asked to prospective jurors at the time jurors were impaneled."[412] Homans also believed that using the services of the Project "would be expensive and that … the cost could in some part whether small or large be partly taken care of through the efforts of the Boston/Boise Committee."[413]

Reeves saw this as an appropriate way for Boston/Boise to contribute to the effort. Financial support of the National Jury Project was meant to ensure that the defendants received a fair trial. "There was such a degree of homophobia in the community," he recalled, "that this was a major issue."[414]

On March 27, 1978, Reeves wrote Homans that the committee

> wishes to sponsor with your client and other of the defendants the involvement of the National Jury Project. To that end, we will gladly receive donations earmarked for that purpose and forward them to you for payment to the National Jury Project *and we will make a contribution from our general fund shortly after April 5* to help toward the $25,000 total cost as indicated in the budget submitted by the NJP...[415] (emphasis added).

The committee soon announced that it would host a benefit and that the featured speaker would be the author Gore Vidal, who was certain to draw a large audience and thereby help fill the committee's coffers. John Mitzel had interviewed the author for *Fag Rag,* and he and Reeves had maintained a correspondence with Vidal. The author was about to begin a speaking and publicity tour in various American cities, and Mitzel and Reeves were able to persuade him to stop in Boston and speak on behalf of Boston/Boise.

Vidal, it turned out, was a bigger draw than anyone could possibly imagine. And so it was that on the morning of Sunday April 2, 1978, as he was reading the *Boston Globe,* Superior Court Chief Justice Bob Bonin saw a notice that Gore Vidal would be speaking the following Wednesday evening at the Arlington Street Church. The notice in the *Globe* did not explain that Vidal's appearance was connected to a fundraiser for the Revere defendants. Bonin asked Angela if she wanted to attend, and she said yes. They agreed to invite some friends and arrange for a dinner after the lecture.

WEDNESDAY APRIL 5, 1978

Bonin was taken by surprise when he and his party arrived at the church and were immediately identified and escorted to choice seats by Joseph Miller, an event organizer. The Boston/Boise Committee had been expecting him. When he purchased his tickets for the event, the chief justice asked whether seats could be reserved and left his business card with a church volunteer, Laura Campbell. Bonin had asked Campbell about

Boston/Boise when he purchased the tickets, and she did not mention that the lecture was also a fundraiser.[416] Campbell subsequently alerted the event's organizers that the chief justice was planning to attend the lecture. Dermot Meagher, who was in the audience, recalled nudging his friend Vincent McCarthy and whispering "That's Chief Justice Bonin," and McCarthy—a lawyer with Hale & Dorr—replied "What's he doing here, the fool?"[417] When Miller asked Bonin if he would like to be introduced, Bonin replied, "No, I'm just here to hear Gore Vidal."[418]

John Mitzel introduced Gore Vidal to the crowd gathered in the Arlington Street Church with a call to arms: "We're working against some very powerful prejudices and some very powerful people who would see us crushed and are doing their best to create a climate like the witch hunt … and the way things have been going the last few weeks, I don't think it's inappropriate to characterize what's coming down as nearly a state of siege against the gay community and anyone interested in civil liberties."[419]

Mitzel followed Tom Reeves, who had spoken at length about the Revere cases. "We are not defending child molesters," said Reeves. "I've met the boys and the men and I know that

Figure 8: Stone of Stumbling
Bob and Angela Bonin share a light moment at the Gore Vidal lecture
in the Arlington Street Church. Angela Bonin would remember that
"things got grim really fast."

Figure 9: "It's Wrong To Assume Judges Are Troglodytes"
Chief Justice Bonin meets Gore Vidal after Vidal's Arlington Street
Church lecture.

what we're dealing with is a human situation of good affectional relationships between men and boys in most of these twenty-four cases. We are proud to be representing the group of men, among the twenty-four, who deserve a fair trial and a hearing and that's all we're asking for."[420] Taking aim at the district attorney, Reeves said that "in an election year the popular thing is to go out and 'get the gays' because that will get the vote, and this is an election year for certain people that we know—Mr. Byrne and others—and they still think that's the way America works."[421]

Gore Vidal lightened the mood when he finally took the stage, sparking laughter when he claimed to have enjoyed neither sex nor politics in Massachusetts—and that therefore he was "able to bring distance if nothing else to this program."[422] But it was quickly clear that Vidal had been briefed on the advocacy of the Boston/Boise Committee on behalf of the Revere defendants. "Everyone wants to protect our children," said Vidal, "so there is an instinct that this is very good politics."[423] Vidal waded not so gently into the area of intergenerational sex. "There is a difference, believe it or not, between child and adolescent. The word adolescent seems to me to be lost around here. I would say that puberty is a dividing line and it's a very delicate area."[424]

"Coercion is a delicate subject," opined Vidal. "Much complaint has been made about men and boys. Well, 'the man's in the stronger position. The boys have a weak character or can be modeled by a man.' This is not necessarily so. Relations have to be very subtle. Who does the manipulation is a quite delicate matter and one that I think the state would be well-advised not to involve itself in."

Vidal cast the real villains as the parents of the adolescents, and the district attorney. "If parents are worried about their children, well they should have done the work in the family and not suddenly find themselves in the position of having a witch hunt and re-invoking the spirit of nearby Salem," he said. And then he took on Garrett Byrne: "district attorneys ought not to be allowed to have a hotline so that anybody can call up and say who's a witch and who was last seen with Goody Bellows down on the Common." The author made clear his contempt for "those who are so intent on saving children [but] don't mind in the least putting them in reform schools where they get raped and beaten up quite regularly. They don't mind that at all. But a consenting relationship they think to be a bad thing."[425]

It would be incomprehensible later for many that Bob Bonin, listening to these speeches, did not get up and leave the church. In fact, the chief justice was paying little attention to the warm-up speakers. "It sounds stupid to say that I was not being attentive to [Tom Reeves's] remarks," Bonin recalled some years later, "but I certainly didn't go to the lecture to hear Tom Reeves."[426] Angela Bonin referred to the event as very "discombobulated," and their friend Tom Lambert later testified that the speeches were made in an "atmosphere . . . of confusion."[427]

Bonin tuned out Reeves, but he certainly listened to Vidal—and he didn't like what he was hearing. Bonin remembered feeling that he "disagreed with Vidal's view that if an adult man is having sexual relationships with a mature fourteen-year-old boy, that it's not so bad. How would the fourteen-year-old give consent?"[428] Bonin would later admit to hearing "polemics expressed against the district attorney's office" while seated in the church. "One could say that when they were voiced I should have gotten up and walked out. I considered that, but then I don't know, maybe it was stubbornness, I felt the best thing to do would be to stay and listen gracefully."[429]

The evening turned out to be a disappointment for Bonin, his wife and their guests. They had hoped to hear a lecture by Gore Vidal on a topic of some general interest, and instead found themselves in the midst of a highly charged political rally, and listening to the famous author defend intergenerational sex. It was not what they had expected, but they remained in the church throughout the evening, and after the lecture Bonin spoke with Vidal and asked him to autograph his copy of Vidal's historical novel, *Burr*.

Bob Bonin was not prepared for what greeted him at the Arlington Street Church. He was even less prepared for the tidal wave of bad press and rancor that would follow—a tidal wave that would sweep him out of office.

THURSDAY, APRIL 6, 1978

The headline on page one of the *Boston Herald American* the next day screamed: "Bonin at benefit for sex defendants." Above the headline was a photograph of the chief justice and his wife, seated in the church, and appearing amused at something being said. The lead paragraph explained the problem in plain terms:

> Massachusetts Superior Court Chief Justice Robert M. Bonin was among some 1,500 persons attending a benefit meeting in Boston last night to raise funds for a "fair trial" of twenty-four men indicted on sex charges involving boys

eight to thirteen years old. Bonin, in his capacity as chief
justice, will be responsible for appointing judges to preside
at the trials.

And on page three, in case anyone missed the point, was a
photograph of Bonin and Vidal together.[430] Playing catch-up
in its evening edition, the *Boston Globe* printed a page one
story filled with quotes from unnamed sources who believed
that the chief justice's appearance at the event "would require
re-opening the investigation into Bonin's judicial conduct."[431]

Tom Reeves, reading the *Herald American* that morning,
burst out laughing. "I thought it was the funniest thing I had
ever seen in my life," he said. "Wow. We made it to a new
level!" Suddenly, Boston/Boise was front-page news. Reeves
recalled, "This is a weakness of political radicals—we so seldom
get the media at all that if they are there we certainly aren't
going to throw them out the door." Although they had not
expected much media coverage of the event, Reeves and his
cohorts were delighted at the attention. Then Reeves had a
second thought, this time about Bob Bonin: "Who's out to get
this man?"[432]

Reeves's question was spot on, because the photographer

sent to the Arlington Street Church was not there by accident. *Herald American* photographer Mike Andersen, who took the two photographs that helped spark the furor, was sent to the church by his photo assignment editor, John J. Landers, Jr., acting on a tip. The mini-drama being played out that evening at the *Herald American* is, in itself, a lesson in how the press can shape the course of events even while it is being silently manipulated by the hidden agendas of skillful men.

The *Herald American,* like all newspapers, functioned off a "daily budget"—an allocation of pages and stories that formed the framework of the next day's paper. The Vidal lecture was listed on the April 5th daily budget for publication the next day, but no reporter was assigned to cover the event, and photo assignment editor Landers was prepared to use a stock photo of Vidal if the event remained in the budget. Sometime during the afternoon of the lecture, *Herald American* reporter Tom Sullivan was tipped off that Bonin would be attending the lecture. Sullivan was well known and liked by the courthouse crowd—he was the kind of reporter who, in Andersen's words, "not only made contacts, he made friends." Tipped off by such a "friend," Sullivan penciled a notation on the daily budget: "Judge Bonin has bought four tickets."[433]

When Landers saw Sullivan's notation, he brought it to the attention of City Editor Norman Gray. A decision was made to send Mike Andersen to the church to record Bonin's attendance. Andersen had taken Bonin's photograph before, but he did not remember what the jurist looked like. As he looked out on a sea of men in the church, Andersen worried to himself that he had no certain way to identify Bonin. Then he noticed a tall man with a salt and pepper beard walking down the aisle, accompanied by a beautiful blond woman. Angela Bonin was unmistakable, and Andersen knew he had his man.

Andersen had a difficult time taking a good photo of Bonin. The lighting in the church was low, and the high ceiling made use of a flash unhelpful. Andersen also felt that he was "conspicuous enough without popping a flash every few minutes." Despite the technical challenges, he managed to get a decent grainy photo of Bob and Angela seated in the audience, and he later got a better photograph of Bonin and Vidal together at the post-lecture reception.[434]

Back at the *Herald American* there was a sense of urgency about getting Andersen's photographs in time to make the morning newspaper. Landers called Andersen on his two-way radio, informing him that his colleague Rollie Oxton would drive over to the church to pick up Andersen's film. By the time Oxton got the photos to the *Herald American,* they were too late to make the paper's first edition. The photos and a short unsigned story did make it to the paper's final edition, which was the edition most likely to be picked up by Boston residents the next morning.[435]

The question remains: who tipped the *Herald American* that afternoon regarding the possibility of Bonin's attendance at the lecture? Who would want Bonin's attendance memorialized in the morning newspaper? Andersen did not know who Sullivan's courthouse source was, but as the drama unfolded it would become clear that two men in the courthouse, Bonin's assistants Frank Orfanello and Francis Masuret, knew that the chief justice was planning to attend the Vidal lecture, and one of them—Orfanello—knew the incendiary fact that the lecture was also a fundraiser.

The matter raised an emotional and visceral public outcry. It was as if all of the forces that could possibly be arrayed against him were poised, simultaneously, to respond with lightning speed. Bonin's attendance at the Vidal lecture was a spark that ignited a flash fire of opposition. In the middle of the storm, one Boston attorney said that Bonin was "the best lawyer I've ever met, and a man of unimpeachable honesty. But it's a naive honesty. It was clear there were people out to get him, so why the hell did he have to make it so easy for them?"[436] Frank Bellotti, many years later, recalled that Bonin's enemies "were waiting to nail him and he helped them. For a guy who came from Grove Hall he didn't have street smarts. They were going to get rid of him no matter how. They were *looking* for excuses to get rid of him. He wasn't one of their own."[437] Reeves himself "realized for the first time the power of this issue [intergenerational sex] to destroy, absolutely destroy people."[438] Angela Bonin would remember that "things got really grim really fast."[439]

The controversy was not twenty-four hours old before District Attorney Byrne pounced on it, holding a press conference to denounce the chief justice and calling on him to remove himself from any further judicial role in the assignment or trial of the pending Revere cases. It was a predictably impressive display of political savvy on the part of the eighty-year-old Byrne. Byrne accused Bonin of lending "the prestige of his office to advance the interests of the defendants," and suggested that the chief justice might be in violation of the judicial canons of ethics, specifically Canon 2, which provides that "a judge should conduct himself at all times in a manner that promotes public confidence in the integrity and impartiality of the judiciary." Asked why he made reference to the judicial canons of ethics, a matter over which he had no official purview or concern, Byrne responded, "Because it's relevant."[440]

Byrne failed to mention that Canon 5 of the same judicial code permitted a judge to attend an organization's fund-raising events, but he was on to a hot issue, and he was no friend of Bonin's. Three days earlier Bonin's chief nemesis, Walter McLaughlin, had sent a letter to Boston lawyers inviting them to a fundraiser for the district attorney at the trendy new Faneuil Hall Marketplace. The retired chief justice's letter noted that "you and I have a vested interest in insuring the continuation of competence and integrity in the Suffolk County District Attorney's office. During my career, both as a trial attorney and chief justice of the Superior Court, Garrett Byrne has instilled those two characteristics in the vigorous and professional conduct of his office."[441] McLaughlin's decision to raise campaign funds for Byrne was extraordinary—a former senior jurist soliciting campaign contributions for a political figure. It was a clear indication of the strength of the personal ties between the men.

Political contributions were important in any election, and in this campaign against his former first assistant, Byrne needed to raise sufficient funds to mount a sophisticated and effective advertising campaign. His campaign brochures were slick and professional: he was "Garrett Byrne, the man who turned the tide against crime in Suffolk County"; he was "Mr. District Attorney"; he was, above all, "winning his war against sex criminals, pornographers, and Combat Zone flesh peddlers."[442]

FRIDAY, APRIL 7, 1978

The attacks on Bonin did not let up. On Friday, a number of conservative political leaders called for Bonin's removal from the bench. All of the Dukakis/Bellotti enemies came forward in a rush to judgment. Executive Councilor Herb Connolly once again called on Bonin to step down. Gubernatorial candidates Francis Hatch and Edward King, each vying to defeat Dukakis in the 1978 election, called for Bonin's ouster. Hatch, a Republican, took delight in likening Bonin's behavior to "Judge Sirica going to a benefit for G. Gordon Liddy." King, a conservative Democrat who would defeat Dukakis in a surprise primary victory and then go on to defeat Hatch in November, called on Dukakis to "remedy his selection of Justice Bonin promptly and decisively."[443]

The furor was so swift and so great that Bonin believed it necessary to make a public statement, which he did Friday afternoon, April 7. Bonin's statement became the template of his defense throughout the proceedings against him:

> On Sunday, April 2, 1978, I read an announcement in the *Boston Globe* Focus section that stated: "Author Gore Vidal will discuss *Sex and Politics in Massachusetts* Wednesday evening at the Arlington Street Church. Admission is $5.00 and funds will be used to benefit the Boston/Boise Committee." I had read books by Mr. Vidal, had seen him on television, and knew him to be a gifted author and speaker. I purchased tickets on April 3, 1978. The ticket stated *Boston/Boise Committee presents Gore Vidal* together with the time, place and price. Neither the ticket nor the *Globe* announcement stated that the funds were to be used for a defense fund or a statewide poll. I attended the lecture. Shortly before attending the lecture, I learned that the Boston/Boise Committee was part of the gay community. That fact alone did not, nor does it now, present any reason for our not attending. Prior to my attending the lecture, I did

not know that any of the funds from the ticket sales would be used in any defense fund, pending cases or, indeed, for any purpose other than as stated in the *Globe* or on the ticket. In fact, I did not learn of the intended use of these funds until reading in the press on April 6, 1978, the day following the lecture. I had the right to listen to a talk sponsored by a gay rights group. I would never knowingly contribute to a defense fund. Simply stated, I went to a church solely to hear a lecture by an eminent literary figure.[444]

Angela Bonin issued her own statement in defense of her husband: "I am married to a 'public servant,'" she declared. "I never knew that public servant meant having every action as a private person made public… Judges and their families must enjoy the same civil rights as all other people: to assemble, to stand for whatever principle they espouse." Angela concluded her remarks with a call to a broader concern: "A frightened, weakened judiciary is a danger to all of our rights. If a judge cannot attend a lecture by an author in a church, none of us are safe, none of our civil rights are safe."[445]

Angela's statement did not stop there. She continued with a spirited defense of gay rights, declaring that "A support of gay rights is a support of all our civil rights." As far as she was concerned, Angela and her husband stood in defiance of those who could not understand that it was equally important to the appearance of judicial fairness that someone of her husband's rank and position hear the "other side" of a difficult and emotional debate. It was an unorthodox and, to many, courageous position, coming as it did from the wife of the chief justice. But it missed entirely the point that the Arlington Street Church event was not a rally for gay rights in its commonly understood and acceptable form, but a forum organized by a controversial fringe group within the gay rights community, a group whose members espoused a view of sexual freedom that was difficult for many, including most gay people, to embrace. A fundamental question remained unanswered: did her husband know, prior to attending, that the event was a fundraiser for the Revere defendants?

SATURDAY, APRIL 8, 1978

The weekend offered no respite for the Bonins. The Saturday *Boston Globe* called on the chief justice to "clear the air in this situation by immediately assigning all responsibility in connection with the Revere cases to another member of the court."[446] The *Quincy Patriot Ledger* declared that Bonin's attendance at the lecture displayed "an appalling lack of judgment and propriety."[447] And his old opponent, Walter McLaughlin, came out swinging, issuing a blistering statement that was carried in full in the *Herald American*.

McLaughlin took direct aim at Bonin, claiming that the chief justice's appearance at the Vidal lecture "ruptures the very heart of our judicial system, and taints the whole process." And then the former chief justice took on the role of judge, jury and executioner as he passed a harsh public sentence on his successor:

> I have read the statement released by the chief justice. It is incredible that he did not know the nature of the meeting; or, that nobody told him in advance, or that when he arrived and found out the nature of the meeting, he did not walk out. It was sprinkled with prominent defense counsel representing the indicted defendants. He ought not to have been appointed in the first place. He should have resigned four months ago. And, if he does not resign, he should at least have the good sense to suspend himself until his fitness is judicially resolved. He owes that to the integrity of his court.[448]

SUNDAY, APRIL 9, 1978

The Sunday *Herald American* headline said simply, "Bonin's credibility at issue." Indeed it was. The question now was whether he would be given a fair opportunity to defend himself, to explain his actions and exonerate himself, or would the tidal wave of disapproval sweep him prematurely out of office?

Tom Reeves by now could see clearly what was happening. "I had the feeling that our issues were being used and were not the real issues concerning the judge." Reeves recalled. Reeves had spoken with Bill Homans and said, "You know, I don't think we should give any money to the Jury Project."[449] He wrote Bonin a letter explaining that "not one penny has been spent for the defense" of the twenty-four men, "nor will it be. As your ticket stated, the meeting _was_ a benefit. The money (not very much, really) will go for further publicity, further efforts to achieve fair trials for all gay men facing such sentences, and further efforts to break through the unfairness of the media."[450]

Indeed, the committee had decided that given the disappointingly small amount of money raised at the Vidal event, and the controversy surrounding the chief justice, none of the funds raised at the Vidal lecture would be contributed

to the National Jury Project.[451] This decision after the fact—
which represented a complete reversal of Reeves position as
expressed in his March 27 letter to Bill Homans—did not
soften the growing movement against the chief justice. Reeves
stated that he and the committee "believe that a backlash is
growing against Mr. Byrne and against others who would
slander you and other public servants unjustly." He was wrong.

MONDAY, APRIL 10, 1978

Monday was not an auspicious beginning of the new week. In
the *Globe*, veteran columnist David Farrell wrote an op-ed piece
that was distinguished by its thinly veiled anti-Semitism.[452]
Referring in several paragraphs to the chief justice's "chutzpah,"
Farrell opined that Bonin's problems could be traced to "his
very ambitious second wife. She's aggressive and wields an
enormous amount of influence over her husband." Not content
with personal attacks on the chief justice and his wife, Farrell
went further, chastising the state's Supreme Judicial Court for a
"lack of leadership" in not removing Bonin, declaring that the
"prestige of the high court ... has begun to diminish."

Farrell's evidence for this supposed loss of prestige was
nothing less than the court's 1975 decision to re-admit Alger

Hiss to the Massachusetts Bar. A recently published book had accused some of the sitting justices of a predisposition to exonerate Hiss before even hearing evidence on the matter. Farrell complained that the court's "predisposition" to rule on the Hiss case was "in sharp contrast to the current reluctance to take a hard look at the Bonin case." In one column, Farrell had identified Bonin with the negative stereotypes of his religious heritage, attacked his wife, linked the matter to the Alger Hiss affair and its lingering aroma of un-American activities, and challenged the high court's justices to take decisive action with respect to Bonin.

The justices of the state's highest court may well have read Farrell's piece, throwing down the gauntlet to them in no uncertain terms. Either the Supreme Judicial Court would act decisively to remove this chief justice with "chutzpah" and an intolerably assertive wife, or they would suffer the consequences in the editorial pages of the *Globe*. The question was whether they would prove true Gore Vidal's subsequent assessment that "Judge Bonin, as a Jew, did not suit the prejudices of the Roman Catholic-WASP judiciary of the state."[453] The answer was forthcoming. Allan Rodgers, the chairman of the Committee on Judicial Responsibility, responded to a reporter's inquiry by saying "We do read the newspapers and we pay attention to what we read."[454] The Committee on Judicial Responsibility announced that it would investigate the conduct of the chief justice of the Superior Court.

Late on Monday, having spent most of the day huddled with advisors, Bonin voluntarily agreed not to take any cases during the investigation. He would continue to administer the trial court, but he would not perform judicial duties. Bonin's statement was read twenty minutes before midnight by David Sargent, the Dean of Suffolk University Law School and one of Bonin's lawyers. The statement repeated his essential defense: "I did not have any prior knowledge of the use of the funds. I would never knowingly contribute to a defense fund or attend a defense fund function."

Realizing that he had to act decisively or risk losing all, Bonin stated that "in view of the sensational media coverage, and to allay any possible public misconception, I will not participate in or assign any of these cases … and will not assign myself to sit until the committee issues its findings relative to its investigation."[455] Bonin's statement was not enough for those now eager to push the matter to a quick and conclusive end.

In the midst of the growing movement against Bonin, Walter

McLaughlin was a particularly busy man. The press reported that McLaughlin had visited the offices of the Supreme Judicial Court late Monday afternoon "seeking a conference with Chief Justice Hennessey concerning developments in Bonin's case."[456] What the press did not know was that the day before, on Sunday afternoon, McLaughlin had a private meeting with Frank Orfanello, his loyal administrative assistant who had been retained by Bonin. Orfanello had sought out McLaughlin not merely as a friend, but as counsel, which meant that their conversations would be protected by the attorney-client privilege.

On Thursday, Orfanello had given Bonin's lawyers an account of a conversation between him and the chief justice on the day of the lecture. Orfanello's statement to Bonin's lawyers confirmed Bonin's statement that he did not know in advance of the lecture that it was a fundraiser for the Revere defendants. Now, after meeting with McLaughlin, Orfanello was changing his story. The noose was tightening.

TUESDAY, APRIL 11, 1978

Tuesday was a bad day for Bonin, perhaps the decisive moment when the possibility of his removal from office began to take on an aspect of reality, if not inevitability. Two legislative events took place in rapid succession on Monday afternoon, and they hit Tuesday's newspapers like an explosion. First, the Massachusetts Senate voted 29-2 to urge Bonin to suspend himself immediately from all duties as chief justice pending completion of a full investigation by the Committee on Judicial Responsibility.[457] At the same time, at the opposite end of the State House, a member of the House of Representatives declared that if Bonin did not "step aside, I am prepared to file a bill of address to have him removed permanently."[458] This rapid legislative response, and the lopsided Senate vote in particular, "had a stunning impact among supporters of the chief justice as well as on the two attorneys representing him," according to the *Herald American*.[459]

The threat of removal by address, first raised on this day, was a significant event. Address is a constitutional method of removal that, in Massachusetts, requires only a majority vote of the Legislature (in contrast to the two-thirds vote required for impeachment). Moreover, the address does not require a hearing, the development of facts, or any process prior to removal. It is a harsh procedure, used up to that time in the 20th century only in those rare circumstances where a judge had been both suspended from the bench and disbarred.[460]

Invoking the address was a signal that the movement against Bonin had reached a dangerous pitch among state decision makers.

Indeed, veteran State House correspondent A. A. Michelson noted that "the Legislature is loaded for bear … a part of the Legislature would jump at the chance of removing Bonin only to embarrass Gov. Dukakis, who appointed Bonin over violent objections from the court establishment." Michelson reported that Bonin was being "tried … on the campaign hustings. All challengers to Gov. Dukakis, Republican and Democratic, are trying to make the Bonin 'case' an issue."[461]

Governor Dukakis, angry and disappointed with his appointee and facing a tough political challenge of his own, ultimately came to consider removal by address as the quickest, simplest way to put a conclusive end to the matter. But on this Tuesday in April, Bob Bonin still looked upon Dukakis as an ally. Later that day, Bonin delivered a handwritten note to Dukakis, explaining his decision to recuse himself from sitting on cases pending resolution of the Vidal lecture controversy. His action, he explained, "was dictated by public furor. It seemed best to try to calm the situation and minimize interference with judicial administration. I faced conflicting principles involving my judicial responsibility and civil rights. I regret the problems."[462]

It was a day for correspondence. A letter from the justices of the Supreme Judicial Court, signed by Chief Justice Edward Hennessey, was delivered to Bonin in his office on the eleventh floor of the courthouse, "suggesting" that he immediately remove himself from all judicial and administrative duties.[463] The letter was polite, but it was an ultimatum nonetheless. For if Bonin failed to heed the "suggestion" of the state's highest court, what other recourse would they have but to suspend him against his will? Yet removal or resignation was anathema to Bob Bonin, and he would not acquiesce.

WEDNESDAY, APRIL 12, 1978

Bonin responded to Chief Justice Hennessey with his own letter, "respectfully declining" to voluntarily suspend himself from all duties. "I must adhere to my personal principles and be faithful to the serious civil liberties issues involved in my attending a lecture," said the chief justice. He requested a hearing in the event that the court wished "to proceed further."[464]

The SJC immediately honored the chief justice's request, and informed him that they would hold a hearing the next morning on the limited question "whether, without regard to the merits of any matter which is now under consideration by the court's Committee on Judicial Responsibility, the public interest, including the effective administration of the Superior Court and public confidence in fair administration of justice in this Commonwealth, requires such suspension."[465]

The reaction to the exchange of letters by the respective chief justices was immediate and explosive. Governor Dukakis, who had until now maintained his silence, called on Bonin to temporarily vacate his office.[466] Attorney General Bellotti was already on record asking for Bonin's resignation. But Bonin would not resign. With the loss of Dukakis, Bonin was effectively without political allies. Within an hour of the release of Bonin's letter to Hennessey, a bill of address for his removal was filed in the House of Representatives by State Representative Peter Flynn, a conservative Democrat and a supporter of the governor's primary opponent, Edward King.[467]

THURSDAY, APRIL 13, 1978

Thursday was, as the *Herald American* put it, "Showdown day for Bonin." He had brought the battle to the place of last resort, the state's highest court, and Bob Bonin was prepared to go the full measure to save his honor and his job. And why not? Hadn't he offered up enough by voluntarily relinquishing *all* judicial duties pending the results of the investigation? Why was there the need to strip him fully of all duties as chief justice? Was there such a loss in public confidence in his administration of the trial court system that his suspension was required?

It was the ultimate question, for if his mere continuation as chief justice meant that public confidence in the system was at risk, he would never be able to serve again as chief justice, no matter how favorable the facts. If the *temporary* solution meant full removal, the conclusion was inevitable. The "temporary" verdict implied the final outcome in a way so conclusively that he was compelled to fight to the last.

The governor was now against him, and the attorney general. Against him also were the two leading contenders for governor, the former chief justice of the Superior Court, the Suffolk County district attorney, twenty-nine members of the State Senate and a growing majority of the members of the House of Representatives. There was one isolated voice of support from the Boston/Boise Committee. On the eve of Bonin's appearance before the SJC, the committee issued a statement:

> No money from our committee has gone to the defendants
> or their attorneys in any of these or similar cases. The

committee has been a civil liberties and educational group.
Our sponsorship of the National Jury Project involvement
in some of the recent cases does not constitute defense
of individual defendants, but is in line with one of our
original demands: assure fair trials.[468]

The committee was careful to keep its comments low key, and
issued them from its attorney, John Ward. As Committee Co-
Chair Reeves explained it to Bonin, "I have refrained from
overtly supporting you during all this while, knowing that
our infamy would not be helpful."[469] Gore Vidal, watching
these events from a distance, issued a statement that, so far
as he knew, the Boston/Boise Committee was "a civil rights
group. And so, when I read about the Judge Bonin issue I was
rather startled. I never heard of a defense league. My remarks
were of a more general nature. They were in no way specific to
any of these defendants, none of whom I know."[470] He wrote
to Bonin expressing "how sorry I was to have been used as a
pretext to destroy a much-admired jurist."[471]

But the proceedings before the SJC had nothing to do
with sorting out the facts. Chief Justice Hennessey's pointed
limitation of the question before the court as whether public

confidence had been jeopardized—and expressly *not* whether the merits of the case had any substance—meant that the facts were a useless defense for Bob Bonin. Vidal cautioned, "The spirit of Salem once again rises in Massachusetts."[472]

The Massachusetts Supreme Judicial Court in those days presided in a large, solemn room on the thirteenth floor of what was known as the "new" courthouse in Boston, an art deco building in historic Pemberton Square, erected as part of the New Deal program. The high-ceilinged room was decorated simply with dark wood paneling and portraits of former justices. The dark blue carpet was thick, the lighting indirect, the marble around the main doorway black—the whole a masterpiece of official understatement. Behind the bench, which was large enough to accommodate all seven justices at one time, was a dark blue curtain that would be drawn open at the beginning of each session to reveal the judges standing behind.

On this morning the courtroom was filled to capacity with lawyers, reporters and citizen onlookers wanting to witness the day's drama. A few minutes before the proceedings were scheduled to begin, Robert and Angela Bonin entered the courtroom and silence swept over the assembled crowd. Bob Bonin kissed his wife and walked over to his reserved seat at his counsel's table. He turned in his seat and scanned the crowd. It was rare to see the courtroom so full. But this was, or would be, history, and many people came to witness the event. Bob Bonin turned to face the front of the room. It was 11:30 AM Thursday, April 13, and the chief court officer stood to announce the entrance of the justices. The heavy curtains parted, and they entered. It would be over in eighteen minutes.

Paul Sugarman was one of Robert Bonin's two lawyers, and it was his duty this day to present the chief justice's case. Sugarman's résumé was a mirror image of Bonin's; a graduate of Boston University Law School, followed by service in the U.S. Army JAG Corps, and then the private practice of law in a small firm. He enjoyed Bonin's full confidence. His opening statement was neither eloquent nor passionate, but workmanlike in its approach. Reminding the court that there "were not, nor are there now, any charges against [Bonin]. In fact, there are no facts that have been found, preliminary or otherwise," Sugarman opined. "What appears to be happening is that a mood has been created in the face of sensational media coverage." "We submit," said Sugarman,

> that public confidence will in the long run be more seriously
> diminished if a judicial officer of the court is suspended,

even temporarily, without the knowledge of the facts, and without any charge or accusation having been made, because if it occurs, it would be due to a mood and an atmosphere created by those—who had a right to say what they have said—who have not heard all the facts, and by those who react to this atmosphere. That would be an injustice. And we do not subscribe to the philosophy that an injustice must be done to one person for the good of the system. If this be the case, the system is not what it purports to be.[473]

A brief series of questions followed. "You give no credence to an argument that might be made that orderly judicial process might be encouraged and supported by a temporary removal, voluntary or otherwise, of the chief justice?" asked Associate Justice Herbert Wilkins. No, said Sugarman, not "if this type of action is to be taken in the context of the mood without the determination of the facts."

Chief Justice Hennessey asked, "[if] the administration of the Superior Court has now reached a stage of relative impasse, assuming we reach that conclusion, may we not or must we not in the public interest consider that?" Sugarman's reply: "Your honor, if these things occur in a public mood that is created not by the actual facts, and without substantiation of this, then in the long run the system will not be served but in fact will suffer."

Hennessey's response foretold the result: "The objective judgment of this court as to the relative state of the efficiency of the administration [of the courts] is not a mood or an atmosphere, it's a matter of fact, is it not, assuming we came to that conclusion?" Lamely, Sugarman replied, "I don't know upon what facts that assumption would be made. I am not privy to what you refer. It's very difficult for me to answer a question in the abstract, especially this one."[474]

The hearing took eighteen minutes to complete. Two hours later, the high court rendered its decision. The chief justice of the Superior Court was suspended "from the performance of all judicial and administrative functions" on a "temporary" basis. No one really believed, explained *Globe* columnist Ken Hartnett, that Bonin "would tilt toward the defense of those charged [in the Revere sex cases]. It's a matter of appearances, of course, and for that reason Bonin had to go… One has to wonder how Bonin, or anyone in Bonin's position, could have stood up to the media attention that resulted from his decision to hear Vidal give one of his lifeless talks."[475]

The day's drama was not yet over. On hearing the news of her husband's suspension, Angela Bonin appeared in the courthouse press room and made a statement. Pointing out that the Boston/Boise Committee continued to assert that none of the funds raised at the Arlington Street Church event were for a defense fund, Angela Bonin declared her husband's innocence. And then she said:

> Has this world gone mad? Everyone, the Legislature, the judiciary, the executive branch, is scrambling to cover his backside. There are elections to consider. There's court reform to consider … it is easier to join the cry to crucify… Some people will be uneasy today because of this decision. Some few will not sleep well tonight; some may even have bad dreams. But the world will go on for everyone else in this state. Our nightmare will continue for a long time.[476]

Gore Vidal had previously raised the specter of "the spirit of Salem" rearing its ugly head in the Bay State. Angela took the analogy further. "I read years ago Marion Starkey's book, *The Devil in Massachusetts,* which vividly describes the terrible and real witch hunt in 1692 in the name of God and religion. This is two hundred and sixty-six years later and this witch hunt is in the name of justice and the judicial process," said the chief justice's wife.

Angela's reference to *The Devil in Massachusetts* was, in

retrospect, a rich and powerful allusion to the tenor of the times. The personal destruction of her husband was the twentieth-century equivalent of the ostracism and panic of the seventeenth century. In Salem the witchcraft accusations "sprang from the heart of an embattled congregation, and members initially directed their fears against those who were not members—the many 'outsiders' living among them—a classic 'us' against 'them' within a bounded community."[477] In Boston in 1978, the same primal instincts motivated the old guard who perceived their world to be embattled, and who directed their own fears and anxieties against the outsiders—in this case, the Jewish liberal chief justice who dared to attend a lecture at the Arlington Street Church.

CHAPTER 8

Trial

THE SUSPENDED CHIEF justice waited at his Brookline home while the Committee on Judicial Responsibility completed its investigation and made its recommendation. Bonin's mail reflected the divided public opinion. "Dear Mr. Chief Justice," read one, "please don't quit!"[478] Another read "Hang in there."[479] And one letter came with no message but the following words hand written in red ink: "FIGHT!"[480] On the other side of the ledger, there were many intemperate letters. One letter castigated Bonin as "an arrogant Jew."[481] Another assailed the chief justice as "a bum … [who should] go open a deli somewhere and invite all your queers down for a double lox on rye."[482] One simply said, "You are a disgrace. Resign!"[483]

On April 15, the *Herald American* called for his resignation, declaring that it was now "impossible for public confidence in Judge Bonin and the Superior Court to be fully restored, no matter what the ultimate disposition of the official investigation into his conduct."[484] On April 22, the Committee on Judicial Responsibility informed the Supreme Judicial Court of its intention to hold formal proceedings as soon as possible on certain charges against the suspended chief justice.

Bonin and his lawyers reached out to G. Joseph Tauro, the retired chief justice of the Supreme Judicial Court, for advice. After several conversations with Paul Sugarman, Tauro agreed to serve as a "friend of the court" in an effort to resolve the Bonin matter prior to a full hearing before the SJC. On May 24, 1978, Tauro drafted a letter to Bonin's counsel in which he expressed his belief that:

> CJ Bonin's capability and capacity to effectively administer the business and the day-to-day operations of his court have been permanently destroyed [because] the CJ depends largely on public good will, and that of the legislative and executive branches of government and the loyalty and cooperation of the Superior Court justices and supporting personnel. Without this, it is most difficult, if not impossible, for a chief justice to provide proper leadership and render effective service. In the existing circumstance, it would be unrealistic

to believe that CJ Bonin would be the beneficiary of this
assistance, now or in the foreseeable future.[485]

Tauro further expressed his view that Bonin's resignation would
obviate the need for a full blown proceeding before the SJC.
Such proceedings, "if Judge Bonin should decide to resign his
office," would serve "no useful purpose" and "would not be in
the public's _best_ interest."[486] It appears from the correspondence
that Sugarman and Tauro sought to formulate an arrangement
by which Bonin could avoid the rigors of a public proceeding
before the SJC in return for his voluntary resignation. It was
an arrangement that presupposed an adverse outcome for the
chief justice. But Bonin did not believe he had done anything
that would require his permanent removal from office, and he
would not resign. Tauro never signed or sent the draft letter,
and his brief role came to an abrupt end.

Ultimately, nine charges were filed against Bonin by
the Committee on Judicial Responsibility, seven of which
related to the chief justice's attendance at the Vidal lecture.
The remaining two charges arose from Conboy Insurance
Company's payment of the cost of two receptions following
Bonin's swearing in as chief justice, and Bonin's subsequent

hiring of three women as secretaries in the courthouse. He had hired three women who had worked with him in the attorney general's office without any process, leaving himself open to charges of favoritism in hiring. The charges were taken up by the Supreme Judicial Court, and a hearing was held, lasting eight days in June.

The trial of an incumbent chief justice was unprecedented in Massachusetts. The proceedings would be before the full bench of the Supreme Judicial Court, minus Chief Justice Hennessey, who was recovering from minor surgery. Ranking Associate Justice Francis Quirico assumed the role of presiding justice on the panel. Robert Meserve led the prosecution on behalf of the Committee on Judicial Responsibility.

Paul Sugarman and David Sargent represented the chief justice. Recalling the trial years later, Bonin held to the belief that his lawyers had performed as well as they could under difficult circumstances, and that his chief problem was not inadequate legal support but inadequate public relations support. But there was at least one person who thought Bonin's legal team was not up to the task. Angela Bonin recalled believing that "the deck was stacked against my husband … and it was like Bonin going against a division of the army with a couple of guys with popguns. I was displeased with Sugarman because I thought he was ponderous and certainly not an impressive and dramatic court lawyer."[487] She also resented Sugarman and Sargent's efforts to silence her. "[Sugarman] may be highly competent … [but] I felt that there was this big chunk of disapproval from them for what I had done and that they were making sure I didn't have an opportunity to say anything else. I thought that hurt my husband's case."[488] Tension among Angela and her husband's legal team grew so great that Sugarman and Sargent refused to meet with the chief justice at his home, where Angela would be present.[489]

Angela understood the importance of public perception to the outcome of her husband's fate. "We were dealing with two very different, maybe many different things. We have the outcome of the case against my husband, and we have the public perception of the outcome of the case. And I don't think that they were helping the public perception and that was certainly one of the things I was trying to do, get beyond the politicking and let the public know the other part of it."[490]

Given that the preponderance of the charges against him concerned his attendance at the Vidal lecture, there were really two questions before the court: did Bonin have prior knowledge that the event at the Arlington Street Church would be a fundraiser for either the Revere defendants or the National Jury Project, and if he did not, should he have left the church once the underlying purpose of the evening was made clear?

Bonin's position had been squarely stated in his public statement of April 7: "Prior to my attending the lecture, I did not know that any of the funds . . . would be used in any defense fund . . . I would never knowingly contribute to a defense fund." That statement had been corroborated by Bonin's administrative assistant, Frank Orfanello, in a statement given to Bonin's attorneys Paul Sugarman and David Sargent, on April 6. That was also the recollection of Orfanello's deputy, Frank Masuret. On April 11 Masuret wrote a longhand account of what he and Orfanello had discussed after Orfanello had been informed of the Boston/Boise Committee event. In that account, Masuret recalled that Orfanello described the Boston/Boise Committee as a "gay organization," but did not mention that the Vidal lecture was a defense fundraiser.[491] That continued to be Masuret's recollection, and the public reports of the event being a fundraiser were at odds with what he remembered being told by Orfanello.

Orfanello's recollection in particular was crucial to the determination of Bonin's veracity because it was Orfanello who, prior to the event, had been informed by Brian McMenimen, counsel for one of the Revere defendants, that the chief justice had purchased tickets for the Vidal lecture and should be warned away from the affair. McMenimen told Orfanello that Bonin "couldn't possibly know that this is, in essence, a defense fundraiser or else he'd never in a million years go to it."[492] Precisely what Orfanello relayed to Bonin would remain a critical and unresolved element of this final controversy.

Unknown to Bonin, Orfanello was having a change of heart and mind about his April 6 statement to Sugarman and Sargent. Three days later Orfanello sought out his patron, former chief justice McLaughlin. Orfanello and McLaughlin met privately for about ninety minutes on Sunday, April 9, at McLaughlin's Belmont home.[493] Following their meeting, Orfanello wrote down an account of his conversation with Bonin that was fundamentally different from the one he had given Bonin's lawyers three days earlier, and mailed the new account to McLaughlin.

On that busy Sunday, before he met with McLaughlin, Orfanello called Frank Masuret. Masuret told Orfanello, "I'm glad you called ... Something is bothering me. We haven't discussed it at all. For some reason, we haven't discussed it."[494] Masuret and Orfanello agreed to meet later that afternoon, after Orfanello's meeting with McLaughlin. Masuret was troubled by what he was reading in the newspapers. "Certain things were bothering me," Masuret would later testify. "Then Saturday morning, I read the news. When I read the newspaper, I was sitting at my breakfast table, and whatever I read, I got very concerned about something. It just didn't seem to jibe."[495]

What Masuret had read, and what troubled him, was McLaughlin's charge in the Saturday *Herald American* that it was "incredible" that Bonin "did not know the nature of the meeting; or that nobody told him in advance."[496] Masuret knew that Orfanello had been informed about the lecture, but Masuret had never heard that the event was a fundraiser. He also knew of Orfanello's close relationship with McLaughlin, and on this Saturday, reading McLaughlin's diatribe in the *Herald* — especially his comment of surprise that "nobody told [Bonin] in advance"—things "just didn't seem to jibe" for Masuret.

Masuret testified that when they met on April 9, he asked Orfanello: "Frank, when you went in to [see] the chief justice last Wednesday, did you tell [him] all about the funds, the fundraiser? That the funds that were collected at the Gore Vidal lecture were going to be used for the benefit of the defendants charged in indictments in Suffolk County? Did you tell him all of this?"[497] Orfanello, for the first time, asserted that he had specifically told Bonin that the Vidal lecture was a defense fundraiser. Paul Sugarman asked Masuret at the trial: "was this after he [Orfanello] had seen Chief Justice McLaughlin that this conversation took place?" Masuret's answer was: "Yes." Sugarman then asked Masuret whether that was the first time he had ever "heard Frank Orfanello speak about a fundraiser?" "It's the first time in my memory that I heard him say it," testified Masuret.

"The truth," as Marion Starkey had written in her book about the Salem witch trials, "was no longer simple."[498]

The Boston/Boise Committee issued a public statement on April 13, 1978 stating: "The Boston/Boise Committee is not a defense committee for the 24 men indicted last December... No money from our committee has gone or will go to the defendants or their attorneys... Our sponsorship of the National Jury Project ... does not constitute defense of individual defendants, but is in line with one of these original demands: assure fair trials. The Boston/Boise Committee has not given any funds toward the National Jury Project."[499]

This appeared to be at odds with what Reeves had said in his March 27 letter to defense counsel, and in his comments at the Arlington Street Church. During his remarks, Reeves stated "I simply want to say that the minister informs us there are over 1,500 people here and that most of this money will be going to the defense of the witnesses, the so-called victims, the parents and to the National Jury Project, which has entered these cases in order to see that a fair trial can possibly exist. This is ... expensive ... that's why you're here. That's why we had to charge you."[500] Reminded of his words twenty years later, Reeves could only say, "If I said it [that the money was going to a fundraiser] I was wrong." Reeves painted himself as a naïve activist caught up in the moment: "We were certainly swept up in the excitement of the moment—with so many people there, and so much attention, and the chief justice."[501]

Two of the most prominent of the lawyers representing the Revere defendants certainly believed that the lecture was a defense fund. Bill Homans testified that he had received a telephone message from the Boston/Boise Committee informing him that Bonin had purchased tickets for the lecture. "I thought in view of this telephone call and its content ... that we owed it to Chief Justice Bonin ... to advise [him] that this was a fundraiser, the proceeds of which would be used to benefit the defendants in the Revere cases."[502] When asked by

Paul Sugarman whether he "understood from Dr. Reeves that
the Boston/Boise Committee was not a defense fund," Homans
replied: "defense committee." "Defense committee?" asked
Sugarman. "That's what Dr. Reeves said," replied Homans, "It
was hard for me to differentiate, to make the distinction."[503]
Indeed, the distinction was difficult for most observers.[504]

Homans and another defense counsel, Brian McMenimen,
agreed that McMenimen would call Orfanello and inform him
of the potential danger. McMenimen testified that he called
Orfanello between three and four thirty in the afternoon of
April 5—the same day as the lecture—and informed him that
the lecture was for a defense fund.[505] In strangely guarded
language, McMenimen called Orfanello to say that "a certain
jurist who shall remain nameless … is planning on attending
a lecture tonight of Gore Vidal sponsored by the Boston/Boise
Committee." When Orfanello asked about the nature of the
committee, McMenimen said, "Well Frank, there are presently
pending in Suffolk County Superior Court twenty-four cases,
indictments, involving alleged homosexual activity with
children arising out of a house in Revere. The [Boston/] Boise
Committee was formed for the benefit of those defendants and
the lecture tonight is for the benefit of those defendants and

the proceeds of the lecture are going to be used to defray some of the legal costs associated with the defense of these cases."[506] Orfanello agreed to pass the message along to Bonin.

Orfanello did speak to Bonin about the lecture, on that the two men agreed. Orfanello pulled the chief justice out of a meeting, took him aside and spoke with him briefly.[507] Bonin asserted that Orfanello simply told him that McMenimen had called to say that the event was sponsored by a gay rights group.[508] When asked under oath whether Orfanello had said "in any form of words that the money collected at the lecture was to be used for the defendants in the Revere action and the children involved," Bonin replied, "He did not."[509]

McMenimen's testimony appeared to support Orfanello insofar as it appeared clear that Orfanello had been told that the lecture was a defense fund. Two Superior Court judges, Kent Smith and John Meagher, testified that the morning after the lecture Orfanello called them to say that he had informed Bonin that the lecture was a defense fund. But Orfanello's colleague of twenty-six years, Frank Masuret, could not recall that Orfanello ever raised the subject of the defense fund with him in their discussions the day of the lecture, and Bonin specifically denied it under oath. Masuret testified at trial that "the first time that it registered with me that the affair was a defense fund" was after he read the *Herald American* the morning after the lecture.[510]

Orfanello had clearly lied, either to Bonin's lawyers or to McLaughlin and Meserve. His explanation was simple: he did lie on April 6 to Sugarman and Sargent, because he was not under oath at the time and because he feared for his job. Frank Masuret was appalled when he found out that Orfanello was changing his story. Meeting with Orfanello later in the afternoon of the Sunday when Orfanello had met privately with McLaughlin, Masuret testified that it was the first time in his memory that he heard Orfanello mention the event was a fundraiser. The shocking impact of this on Masuret was palpable during his testimony:

> We came back to my house and Frank [Orfanello] was there
> and something came up about the statements and so forth
> and Frank told me that he had—I don't know how to describe
> it, whether he had not completed his statement or it was a
> false statement. I had no idea what he said to me, but the
> statement that was there was not the true statement ... And
> I said "Gee Frank. This is not good. You can't do that." Then

> he said something about that he was not under oath when he
> gave the statement and therefore he was not concerned about
> it. I said "But gee Frank, you just can't do it anyway. You've got
> to straighten it out. You just cannot do it."[511]

Masuret did not sleep that night. He walked into Orfanello's office the next morning and said "You've got to straighten this thing out before it goes any further. Go in and see the chief justice. Go in and straighten it out. If you don't want to go to the chief justice, at least go to his attorneys, but don't let this go any further."[512]

As Orfanello explained it during the trial, Bonin called him into his office the day following the lecture and showed Orfanello the ticket to the Vidal lecture. "This doesn't say anything about the defense fund on it, Frank," Orfanello recalled Bonin saying, "and its important to me that I didn't know that this was for the defense of these defendants. It's important that I only knew that it was for a gay group or a gay affair." Orfanello then testified: "I said, 'If that's what you want me to say, Chief Justice, I'll say it.'"[513] The prosecutor of the case against Bonin, Robert Meserve, asked Orfanello about his original statement to Bonin's lawyers, which made no reference to his advising Bonin that the lecture would be a fundraiser:

MESERVE: *"Was that statement true?"*

ORFANELLO: *"Not absolutely."*

MESERVE: *"Did you deliberately omit from that statement any reference to telling the chief justice that this was for the defense?"*

ORFANELLO: *"Yes sir."*

MESERVE: *"Why?"*

ORFANELLO: *"Because I thought if I put it down there, that the chief justice would see it, that he would know I had breached his so-called confidence and that I'd be fired."*[514]

Meserve then played for the heartstrings with his next question: "How many children do you have, Frank?"[515] Orfanello would later break down in tears on the stand, recalling his fear of being fired by Bonin.[516]

Orfanello's testimony was compelling, but was it true? Orfanello testified that the substance of what he said to Bonin was contained in a note he wrote when he was on the telephone with Brian McMenimen. The note, written in pencil, said "Brian McMenimen, Boston/Boise Committee, ring to raise money for defense of defendants indicted."[517] That note alone, of course, did not prove what he actually told the chief justice, but Orfanello never mentioned the note— claimed not to have recalled having it—until he was faced with testifying under oath at a deposition run by Bonin's lawyers. The circumstances of his finding the note called his veracity into question. Orfanello claimed that he found the note in mid-May, on the morning he was first put under oath by Paul Sugarman to formally record Orfanello's recollection of events. The questioning continued:

MESERVE:　　"How did you happen to find it that day?"

ORFANELLO:　"I was going through my pockets. I keep a lot of scrap paper in there of notes that I had taken in the course of time and I suppose because I was going down to be giving a deposition, I wanted to see what I had. I found this small piece of white paper."

_____

MESERVE:　　"What is your practice with regard to the papers in your pocket when you change your suit?"

ORFANELLO:　"I change papers from suit to suit from day to day." [laughter in courtroom]

MESERVE:　　"Do you read them?"

ORFANELLO:　"Very rarely." [laughter in the courtroom][518]

During cross examination, Sugarman blistered Orfanello with a series of questions that underscored the fragility of Orfanello's testimony. He asked Orfanello to describe what he did with the note after he spoke with Bonin.

ORFANELLO:　"Put it in my pocket."

_____

SUGARMAN:　"And there it remained until I took your deposition?"

ORFANELLO:　"Yes sir."

SUGARMAN:　"In one of your pockets?"

ORFANELLO: *"Yes sir."*

SUGARMAN: *"So from April 5, 1978 when you wrote it and put it in your pocket, up until the time that I took your deposition, you had forgotten that memoranda or note ever existed?"*

ORFANELLO: *"Yes sir."*

SUGARMAN: *"And when you changed your suits every day you kept transferring that memorandum from one pocket to another?"*

ORFANELLO: *"Yes sir."*

SUGARMAN: *"And when you had the alleged conversation, or the conversation you had with Justice Bonin, you had forgotten about the memorandum?"*

ORFANELLO: *"Yes sir."*

SUGARMAN: *"And when you had the conversation with Judge McLaughlin on April 9, 1978, that Sunday, you had forgotten about the memorandum?"*

ORFANELLO: *"That's my memory."*

SUGARMAN: *"And when you spoke to Dean Sargent and myself and gave us a written statement on April 7, 1978, you had forgotten about the memorandum?"*

ORFANELLO: *"Yes sir."*

SUGARMAN: *"And Mr. Orfanello, when Mr. Meserve examined you under oath on April 11, 1978, you had forgotten the memorandum?"*

ORFANELLO: *"I'd say so, yes."*

SUGARMAN:	*"Through all this furor and all this newspaper publicity that you had read and heard, you had forgotten about the memorandum?"*
ORFANELLO:	*"Yes sir."*

SUGARMAN:	*"Are you saying to us that you carried that memorandum around in your pocket through all this furor for six weeks without knowing of its existence?"*
ORFANELLO:	*"Yes sir."*[519]

Orfanello also testified that he had the following colloquy with Bonin the morning after the lecture:

ORFANELLO:	*"I said you him, 'I see you've made the newspapers, Chief.'"*
MESERVE:	*"What did he say?"*
ORFANELLO:	*"He said, 'I saw a piece in the Globe.' I said, 'Well your picture's in the Herald."* [laughter in the courtroom][520]

Bonin could not have said that he "saw a piece in the *Globe*" making reference to his attendance at the lecture because there was no such article in the morning edition of the April 6 *Globe*. The *Globe's* first article on the subject appeared in the paper's evening edition, as a hasty follow up to the story carried that morning in the *Herald American*. Either Orfanello's memory was faulty, or he was embellishing his story.

More interesting was Orfanello's testimony relating to his conversation with McMenimen the day following the lecture. Orfanello stated that McMenimen "was a little bit disturbed that there was a piece in the newspaper, that it showed in the newspaper, and I said to him, my memory, 'Brian, if you knew it, others knew it, implying that –'"[521] Meserve abruptly cut Orfanello off at that point, saying: "Never mind. That's sufficiently explanatory."[522]

Who were the "others" Orfanello had in mind, and what was he implying? That the *Herald American* photographs and story were a planned effort to embarrass the chief justice? *Herald American* photographer Mike Andersen was specifically sent to the Arlington Street Church the night of the lecture because of a tip from a courthouse source.[523] Whatever Orfanello had in mind, Meserve made certain that no one in the courtroom would know, and Sugarman never picked up on the matter.

When asked by Paul Sugarman if he had called McLaughlin on the day after the lecture, Orfanello replied only that he "had no independent memory of it." Sugarman also asked him: "The statement that you made to us Mr. Orfanello, that you only told the chief justice that it was a gay benefit and not that it was a fundraiser, do you say that is false?"

ORFANELLO: *"I would say that that's not the complete truth."*
SUGARMAN: *"A half truth maybe?"*
ORFANELLO: *"Probably, yes sir."*

SUGARMAN: *"Did you consider it to be a lie?"*
ORFANELLO: *"A lie?"*
SUGARMAN: *"A lie."*
ORFANELLO: *"I didn't think so sir, not at that time … I thought I had told you what the chief justice wanted you to hear."*[524]

Masuret never changed his recollection of events. His trial testimony was perfectly consistent with the handwritten statement he had provided Bonin's lawyers on April 11: he did not recall that Orfanello ever mentioned that the lecture was a defense fundraiser: "I have racked my brain trying to refresh my memory," Masuret testified. "I wouldn't say that Frank Orfanello did not tell me that, but I have searched my memory and I cannot actually hear Frank Orfanello telling me anything about a fundraiser."[525]

Meserve turned the courtroom air blue with language filled with negative and intolerant references to homosexuals as he cross examined Masuret:

MESERVE: *"You are a man with how many children, Frank?"*
MASURET: *"Four sons."*

MESERVE: *"Four sons. The idea of homosexuality is an abhorrent idea to you, isn't it?"*

MASURET: *"Yes. I don't approve of it."*

MESERVE: *"When you were a boy growing up, you might have sympathy for people, but your attitude towards homosexuality has always been one of disapproval, hasn't it?"*

MASURET: *"I have never approved of it."*

MESERVE: *"You felt that it was a terrible thing that the chief justice would go to a party sponsored by a gay group, didn't you really?"*

MASURET: *"I thought in my mind this is the last place in the world that the chief justice should be."*

MESERVE: *"You had in mind when you thought that, that there were cases involving such people pending in the Superior Court?"*

MASURET: *"I don't know if the cases ran through my mind at that time."*

MESERVE: *"But you do know now, and you did know then that there were cases pending in the Superior Court involving gays or fairies as we used to call them. Is that right?"*

MASURET: *"Yes."*[526]

Masuret testified that he attempted to speak to Bonin as they were leaving the courthouse together the evening of the lecture. Masuret was nervous, he "didn't know how to do it," and thought that if he "open[ed] the subject up to the chief justice ... I would eventually say 'Well, isn't this put on by gay people?' or 'Isn't this a gay organization?'" As the two men were going down the judge's elevator, Masuret turned to Bonin and said: "But Chief, isn't it strange? Why would people be calling in here? Why would people on the outside be concerned about your going?'… The chief justice said back to me, 'I don't know. I don't know. It's like a dictatorship. It's like Nazi Germany.'"[527]

And with that, Masuret "knew that he was annoyed with my inquiry or my further inquiry and I backed right down and I didn't pursue it."[528]

CHAPTER 9

Error

T HE TRIAL LASTED eight days. There were two distinctly different views in the legal community regarding whether Bonin's appearance at the lecture was inappropriate. Was Justice Felix Frankfurter's admonition correct, that "History teaches that the independence of the judiciary is jeopardized when courts become embroiled in the passions of the day"?[529] Or was it appropriate—even essential—for judges to attend public events like the lecture? This point was made by the Civil Liberties Union of Massachusetts in an Amicus Brief: "Public confidence in the courts, we submit, would be enhanced by the appearance of judges" [at] "public meetings where controversial matters are to be discussed."[530]

On July 8, 1978, the Supreme Judicial Court issued its opinion. The court found that "the gift of the leased automobile and the payment by Conboy of the cost of the State House reception and of the dinner ... are not violations [of the canons of ethics] as alleged."[531] However, the hiring of three secretaries did constitute a violation of the canons insofar as their prior work or personal relationship to Bonin gave the appearance of favoritism in courthouse hiring.[532] That left the six charges related to the Vidal lecture. The court outlined what, "in the opinion of a majority of the court, remains unproved."[533] It was *not* proved, said the court:

- that the chief justice actually knew or understood before he attended the meeting at the Arlington Street Church … that the meeting would be a fund raiser for, or would concern itself specifically with, the Revere cases pending in the Superior Court;
- that [Orfanello] succeeded in making either [Mr. Masuret or the chief justice] aware that the meeting would be of that character;
- that the chief justice … sought to have Mr. Orfanello make a statement which the chief justice knew would be false or misleading if made;
- that the chief justice knew the press release was false when issued;
- that the chief justice knew … that [his testimony under oath] was false in any material particular.[534]

Indeed, "any discrepancies between the testimony and the facts can be accounted for by the chief justice's inattention or uncertain memory."[535] The majority of the specific charges against Bonin, specifically the charges of perjury and subornation of perjury, were in the opinion of the court majority, not proved after eight days of trial testimony. But the court was not prepared to exonerate the chief justice.

While Bonin "took some measures to moderate the public reaction … they were not as prompt or as effective as they should have been."[536] It was "the unanimous opinion of the court that the chief justice's behavior was improper," because, "if knowing conduct would be an impropriety, then it seems to the court that it was likewise an impropriety, although a lesser one, for the chief justice, in his impatience or rashness, to fail to take heed of information and warnings which would have brought more definite knowledge to him if he had considered or pursued them seriously."[537]

The court determined that "what was put in jeopardy by this neglect was the impartiality demanded of judges, as well as the appearance of impartiality, also demanded of them… There can be little doubt that the episode had … a negative effect on the confidence of the thinking public in the administration of justice in the Commonwealth."[538] Although the court agreed that Bonin did not "renounce or forgo" his constitutional rights of assembly and speech simply because he was a judge, the "special factor or difficulty in the present case—the stone of stumbling—which did call for caution was that the chief justice had good reason to infer that the particular meeting would trench on matters pending in his court; and so it did in fact. That called for a measure of abstention on his part."[539]

The court censured Bonin because his "conduct was improper and created the appearance of impropriety, bias, and special influence. A judge, particularly a chief justice, must be sensitive to the impression which his conduct creates in the minds of the public. The chief justice has manifested an unacceptable degree of insensitivity to those special obligations which are imposed on a person in his position."

Several justices chose to write separate opinions, reflecting the deep divisions generated by the case. Perhaps the most insightful comments came from Justice Robert Braucher, who joined in the majority opinion "as far as it goes."[540] Braucher hit the problem square on the head by observing that Orfanello's "memory was not always accurate. He had been appointed administrative assistant by the chief justice's predecessor in office, who had vigorously opposed and publicly denounced the appointment of Chief Justice Bonin. The chief justice did not have a high regard for the administrative assistant he had inherited, and Mr. Orfanello was aware of that fact and was concerned about his tenure. The two did not communicate easily and freely."[541] The difficult, tenuous and mistrustful relationship between these two men was, as Braucher aptly noted, at the core of the entire episode.

The public censure was not the end of the matter. The court departed from precedent and took the unusual step of telegraphing its expectation that the governor or the Legislature would take matters further. The court had the power to censure a judge, suspend him from office, and disbar him from the practice of law. But the court had no power to remove a judge. The court therefore deemed it "appropriate … that the suspension of the chief justice should extend for a reasonable time to permit the executive and legislative branches to consider, if they wish, the question of the continuance of the chief justice in office, on the basis of such factors as they think appropriate, including, perhaps, the record before us and the conclusions we have drawn from it."[542]

If the governor and the Legislature would follow long standing precedent, the matter would have ended with the censure. The facts presented by the Bonin case did not lead inexorably to removal of a judge.

Five years earlier, the Legislature had rejected a petition for the address of Superior Court Judge Vincent Brogna, who was implicated in a scandal in which he and a fellow judge, Edward DeSaulnier, were accused of fixing a larceny case. A man accused of larceny approached a bail bondsman who was also a friend of Judge DeSaulnier, offering payment of sixty thousand dollars if DeSaulnier would take action to ensure that his larceny case was favorably disposed of. DeSaulnier contacted Judge Brogna, who was hearing the matter, and Brogna listened "without objection" to DeSaulnier's attempt to influence the case. Brogna heard some preliminary motions related to the matter, but did not sit on the case when it came for trial.

DeSaulnier was suspended from the bench and disbarred, and he thereupon resigned his office. Brogna was given a public censure for his failure to report DeSaulnier's attempt to influence him. The Legislature met in Joint Special Committee to consider whether to remove Brogna, and concluded that the mere fact of public censure by the Supreme Judicial Court did not prove unfitness to hold judicial office. Brogna continued to serve on the bench.[543]

Two years later, Dorchester District Court Judge Jerome Troy was suspended and disbarred by the SJC for, among other offenses, committing perjury in an effort to defraud an insurance company, pressuring an attorney who appeared in his court to give a political contribution to a candidate for governor, and dispensing favorable treatment to clients of lawyers who had performed free legal work for his private business interests. Unlike DeSaulnier, Troy refused to resign after suspension and disbarment. The Legislature took up a petition for address. After decisive votes to remove Troy in both branches of the Legislature, the governor endorsed the petition.[544]

In 1975 District Court Judge Francis Larkin was censured after it was shown that he personally delivered an envelope containing one thousand dollars in cash to the home of the incumbent governor on the weekend before the general election in which the governor was a candidate for re-election. The judge claimed that the cash came from family members, not from him or his wife. The money was returned at the governor's direction. The court censured Larkin, and there was no attempt to remove him.[545]

Finally, Boston Municipal Court Judge Francis X. Morrissey was censured in 1974 for making inquiry of the United States

Attorney with respect to a federal case that had been brought against a friend of the judge's. Morrissey, according to the SJC, had "demonstrated insensitivity" to the canons of ethics, a "careless disregard of the requirement that a judge's conduct be such as to avoid even the appearance of impropriety."[546]

The record, then, is that in the decade prior to the Bonin censure, there had been three judicial censures (Brogna, Larkin and Morrissey), none of which concluded in a removal by address or impeachment. Only in one case, where the judge was suspended and disbarred (Troy), was removal by address deemed an appropriate consequence of the court's action. It was, therefore, a clear departure from established precedent when Governor Michael Dukakis filed with the Legislature a petition for the removal of Chief Justice Bonin by address.

Removal by address was controversial because it deprived its target of the traditional rights of fair hearing and due process afforded in an impeachment proceeding. Moreover, address only required a majority vote of the Legislature, unlike the two-thirds vote required for removal by impeachment. WEEI radio observed in an editorial that "while it may make sense to use address when, say, a judge has been disbarred, in other cases impeachment is the logical route." Bonin's case, in WEEI's editorial opinion, "was not an open and shut case for removal."[547]

The big question now was whether the court's invitation to the governor and the Legislature would be used to force Bonin's resignation. Removal by address had been abused in the past—most notably in the mid-nineteenth century to remove Suffolk County Probate Court Judge Edward Loring. Loring was also a United States Commissioner, and his enforcement of the Fugitive Slave Act was highly unpopular in abolitionist Massachusetts. When Loring enforced the Act to return Anthony Burns, a twenty-year-old slave from Virginia, to his master, popular opinion was swift and strong.

A bill of address was filed in the Legislature seeking Loring's removal. Twice the Legislature voted to remove the judge, and twice the governor rejected the address. In 1858, with the election of a new governor, the address was passed a third time and signed. Loring's removal was deemed appropriate because his enforcement of the Fugitive Slave Act was of "general offensiveness to the community."[548] The minority report opposing Loring's address noted that removal on the grounds stated meant that the "independence of the judiciary [is] at the mercy of temporary caprice or partisanship," and that judges were now dependent upon "public sentiment of the hour."[549] One hundred and twenty years later, Bob Bonin's future also depended upon the public sentiment of the hour.

CHAPTER 10

"Not Luck, But the Triumph of Justice and Reason."

T HERE WERE A FEW EXPRESSIONS of support for Bob Bonin. In a particularly moving letter, a citizen wrote to the chief justice that the "treatment afforded you by the media has been deplorable... I wish you not luck, but the triumph of justice and reason... Be strong."[550] Such words of encouragement were rare. WBZ Television and Radio urged Bonin to step down because he had, in their view, lost all ability to credibly administer the court system. The editorial was sent to Bonin by WBZ editorial director Harry Durning with a short note: "sent with regrets."[551] *Globe* columnist David Farrell had predicted Dukakis's reaction to Bonin's difficulties when he wrote that "one of the criteria by which the voters will decide the governor's re-election credentials will be Bonin's performance."[552]

For Dukakis, who was beginning to see his lead over challenger Edward King erode as the Democratic primary drew near, swift and firm action against Bonin was a predictable, and perhaps sensible, political reaction.[553] "He exercised very poor judgment, the court censure in effect confirmed that, and I thought it was time to end it," recalled Dukakis. "It was sad … you don't enjoy this kind of thing, but it seemed to me that his effectiveness had been severely compromised. The best course would have been for him to voluntarily step down, but he refused to do so."[554]

Nine days after the SJC issued its opinion, Governor Dukakis issued a Proclamation calling the Legislature into special session because the "welfare of the Commonwealth requires that the General Court consider the removal from office of Robert M. Bonin, Chief Justice of the Superior Court."[555] On July 19, the governor's Executive Council approved the request for a special session. The following day, Bonin held a press conference to dispel rumors that he was about to resign. He did "not intend to resign," he said.

The issue according to the chief justice was: "not what is good for me or the 'system.' The issue under the [state] Constitution is whether there has been misconduct justifying removal." Because judges "hold office during good behavior," Bonin concluded that removal was constitutionally inappropriate because "there has been no impeachable offense or misconduct. The real issue here is moral and intellectual, not political. I am not staying on because it is easy; it is hard. I am not being arrogant or stubborn in standing up for what I believe. I attended the Vidal lecture and hired the three secretaries. On other charges I was exonerated... I received the public censure and have, with my family, suffered for eight months. This is punishment enough."[556]

But a majority in the Legislature did not agree.

The Joint Committee on the Judiciary conducted a public hearing on July 25, and Bonin appeared in an effort to make one final plea that removal from office was too harsh a sanction. He went through each of the charges against him and explained his side of the story. The *Globe* reported that Bonin had displayed a "new public humility in the fight for his career," as he apologized for "errors in judgment."[557] Bonin asserted that since the charges of perjury and subornation of perjury had been rejected by the SJC decision, his only offense was acting so as to give the appearance of impropriety. That, in and of itself, and the court's public censure did not in Bonin's view require removal from office.

He wanted to return to the court and determine whether he

could lead. "If I cannot effectively lead or serve, I will resign... I shall voluntarily resign without further hounding or urging. But that is really for me to see and assess under Constitutional tenure, and if I resign, to do so free of the taint of threat."

The Judiciary Committee was not persuaded. The majority report, signed by each of the Senate members except the Senate chairman, and by thirteen of the fifteen House members, declared that the "only question ... is whether it would be in the public interest for both Houses of the Legislature to address the governor requesting the removal of Robert M. Bonin." The majority concluded that "it could not with clear conscience agree in every instance with the court's conclusions based on [the] facts, and holding itself to "to a standard of preponderance of the evidence," the majority reached conclusions about the facts and the veracity of witnesses that went well beyond the majority opinion of the court.[558]

Without the benefit of new or independent evidence, the committee majority interpreted the court's majority and concurring opinions to reach its own separate conclusions, all to the distinct disadvantage of the chief justice. The majority report included as reasons supporting removal specific charges determined by the court not to have been proven (Bonin's knowledge of the nature of the Vidal lecture), or specifically judged by the court not to be a violation of the rules of ethics (the Conboy dinner party and Angela's leased automobile). These findings, which went well beyond those made by the SJC after eight days of testimony, demonstrated the perils of the address, which did not require any fact finding process.

The minority report noted that the court found Bonin culpable only on two grounds, the appearance of impropriety in hiring three secretaries, and in not acting prudently with respect to the Vidal lecture:

> This fact is vital to determining appropriate action by the Legislature since public clamor has obscured what is essential for the Legislature to recognize that the findings against the chief justice of the court are minor in comparison with the allegations of misconduct against him… The link between his attendance at the lecture, and the ultimate disposition of the cases is exceedingly weak. Removing a judge for attending a lecture would have a chilling effect on the first amendment rights judges enjoy to the same degree as do other citizens. The sanction of removal from office consequent upon a censure by the Supreme Judicial Court absent a disbarment order would establish a dangerous precedent and a very low threshold requirement for removal from office. Every precedent is to the contrary.[559]

The minority noted that Bonin's "appointment generated considerable resentment among his colleagues on the Superior Court because he was an 'outsider,' not having previously served as an associate justice of that court... To act favorably on the bill of address would establish an extremely dangerous constitutional and legal precedent for the future. History will judge us harshly if we do so."

Bonin and his lawyers vehemently opposed use of the address to remove him. Their main argument was that the address failed to offer the opportunity for full explanation of events through trial testimony that would be the case with an impeachment proceeding. The address in their view, by its failure to guarantee the basic due process protections inherent in impeachment proceedings, was a threat to judicial independence and fair play. But no one was listening.

The bill of address moved quickly. The House voted 206 to 17 to remove the chief justice.[560] In the Senate, a drama of a different sort was taking place. Senate President Kevin Harrington, implicated in a state building construction bribery scandal, resigned his office on July 31. That same day, the Senate selected a new president, William Bulger of South Boston, whose inaugural address included an expression of gratitude to his constituents and colleagues, and the acknowledgment that "our relationship is based on lifelong friendships."[561]

Bob Bonin's public career was not based on lifelong friendships. Not one person in political power had the incentive or inclination to make an effort to stop the process that was leading to his removal. On August 1, as the first item taken up during Bulger's long and often controversial presidency, the Senate voted 24 to 6 to remove Bonin. A motion to take notes of the Senate debate, and a subsequent motion to collect and print the remarks of the Senators during debate, were defeated, and there remains no official record of the remarks made during the Senate debate.

When the bill of address reached the governor's desk, on the afternoon of August 1, 1978, Dukakis indicated he would approve it. "Well you know, if you're up on that white horse, you're going to fall off with a much larger thump than if you are not," said Dukakis. "I saw my job as governor in the mid-seventies to be, among other things, trying to set some very high standards for both integrity and performance, and I expected the people I picked to meet those standards, and maybe I tended to be overly harsh about people that didn't. This particular job — it was just so visible, so important...

There wasn't any room for poor judgment. No room for poor judgment. This was an appointment for life. And that's what I think was so disappointing about this."[562]

With no options left, with no support from any political quarter, Robert Bonin submitted his resignation. He wrote to the governor on August 2:

> The Legislature has spoken. The approval of the address was unjust and is a bad precedent. Address, without required reasons and trial is a dreadful procedure lacking in due process... I cannot conceive of address for the impropriety of "neglectful" attendance at a lecture and for the appearance of favoritism in hiring secretaries. The media played a major role: they thoroughly pre-tried me... My professional reputation may have been damaged, but my integrity is intact. As Socrates stated in his Apology, "I have never intentionally wronged anyone, although I may not have been able to convince you of that... I am not angry with my accusers or my condemners ... they have done me no harm, although neither meant to do me any good; and for this I gently blame them."[563]

Dukakis immediately accepted Bonin's resignation, with regrets for his "personal difficulties."[564] In a statement following his resignation, Bonin noted that it had been "a long haul starting with my predecessor's incessant raucous blasts to today. Jacob Bronowski notes of Galileo's trial in 1633, 'every political trial has a long hidden history of what went on behind the scenes.' So here." Underscoring Bonin's point on that same day State Senator James Kelly was quoted observing that Bonin was removed "not because of evidence but because he was never welcome and was arrogant."[565]

In a letter to Gore Vidal, Bonin wrote that he believed himself guilty of several "misjudgments, but none so rash as underestimating the extensive and intensive aspects of homophobia and anti-Semitism."[566] Vidal responded to Bonin shortly after the resignation that he "thought your farewell to the troops both dignified and precise. Anti-Semitism and homophobia are powerful elements… Think of this recent business as not a coda but a prelude."[567] Vidal's upbeat words were encouraging, but they belied one harsh reality of the politics of personal destruction. This was no prelude. Bonin never again participated in public affairs.

EPILOGUE

Angela Bonin, in her last press conference, had said that their "nightmare would continue for a long time." It was a reflection, she said later, of her "own private pain."[568] She was in many ways naïve about the impact her husband's selection as chief justice would have on them. "I guess neither one of us really realized that if you're going to be a judge or a chief justice, that you have to live your lives according to other people's standards," she said.[569] Years later, she recalled that the events of 1978 "changed our lives. It changed my husband's personality. This funny, happy, outgoing, 'got the world by the tail' guy became a more somber, more defensive, more hurt person."[570]

Life went on.

Superior Court Justice James Lynch, who had opposed the central reform recommendations of the Cox Committee and was the insider favorite to become chief justice in 1977, was appointed to replace Bonin. Ironically, on July 18, 1978—just ten days after the SJC decision censuring Bonin—the governor signed into law the Court Reorganization Act. The Act was important, and helped resolve the serious funding issues that plagued the court system, but it was a tame step forward in the effort to consolidate and improve the management of the court system. It created seven trial court departments, to be managed by a new chief administrative justice.[571] The governor and the legislature could now take credit for a significant court reform measure, but the reality was that the Court Reorganization Act had significant limitations. The Cox Committee recommended that the Probate, Housing and Land courts be consolidated for administrative and jurisdictional purposes under a single Superior Court chief justice appointed by the governor. Instead, the Court Reorganization Act provided for a new chief administrative justice who would be chosen not by the governor, but by the judges themselves. This was an effective way to ensure that whoever was chosen would be a member of, and fully acceptable to, the club of standing jurists.[572] Underscoring the tame nature of the Act, the legislature went out of its way to note in a preamble that while the new law expanded the powers and responsibilities of certain courthouse personnel, it did not "in any way" impair "the tenure and existing powers and authority of such personnel."[573]

Michael Dukakis lost the Democratic primary for governor in 1978 to Edward King, a loss his wife Kitty frequently described as a "public death." Tenacious as ever, he spent four years rebuilding his image and repairing political fences, and returned in 1982 to defeat King and serve two additional terms. As the Democratic nominee for President in 1988, he won 45.6 percent of the vote (and 111 electoral votes) in defeat to George Bush.

Garrett Byrne lost the Democratic primary in 1978 to Newman Flanagan by a substantial margin.[574] Byrne's prominent role in the Revere indictments could not stem the rising tide against him. The Boston/Boise Committee marshaled forces against Byrne, and believed that they had a hand in his defeat. John Mitzel gloated, "We get to claim that one. You take whatever you can get."[575] The truth was that in an election year that was not kind to incumbents, Byrne's age and inability to keep up with the times caught up with him. The great irony was that he was defeated by his former protégé, the man who made his reputation working as Byrne's trusted assistant on the Edelin case.

Byrne's forced retirement lasted over a decade. In his last

years, the old man would receive visitors and reminisce about the days when politics defined who you were, and who you would become—a rough and punishing calling, but one that could offer a lifetime of security and the chance to wield much power.[576] Politics did that for Garrett Byrne, and when he died in 1989 at age ninety-one, the political and legal establishment gathered in force to honor his memory.[577] Five years later, Walter McLaughlin died, aged eighty-seven.

Some members of the Boston/Boise Committee reorganized themselves to become the North American Man/Boy Love Association, a controversial group that continues to exist on the fringe of society. Tom Reeves stayed in Boston, and settled in to a secure teaching post at Roxbury Community College. He retired in 2001. John Mitzel managed a gay and lesbian bookstore, and when it closed, opened his own "GLBT" store in defiance of the inexorable demise of independent bookstores.

Frank Orfanello was, in the eyes of many who knew him, a gentle soul of a man. It is easy to understand how vulnerable he would be to strong-willed men like Walter McLaughlin. Orfanello remained in his position at the courthouse until his retirement. In 1992 the Supreme Judicial Court suspended him from the practice of law for three months for violating the canons of ethics for attempting to influence a judge in a criminal case. Orfanello had approached Boston Municipal Court Judge Dermot Meagher, hoping, in the court's words, "to influence the merits of the case that was to be tried before Judge Meagher." "I had a message, and I delivered the message," said Orfanello. In yet another demonstration of the close connections that remained in Boston, Orfanello's counsel was Thomas Dwyer, a prominent defense attorney and former protégé of Garrett Byrne. The court found that it "was grossly improper for such communication to have been made," and censured and suspended Orfanello.[578] He died six years later, on July 11, 1998.

Bob Bonin considered leaving Massachusetts and starting over in another state where his notoriety would not follow him. No suitable prospect ever turned up, and after a period he joined the practice of law again with his former law partner Lawrence Zalcman. Bonin held no lasting grudge against Dukakis, who had demanded his resignation, and voted for the governor in his re-election bid, and in subsequent elections.[579] His law practice prospered.

Responding to a reporter's inquiry in 1982, Bob Bonin pondered on the events that removed him from the bench. "If I knew it was going to be treated the way it was," he said of his attendance at the Vidal lecture, "and if one holds the position that public officials should not do things to undermine public confidence in them, then I wouldn't have gone. I don't believe I did anything wrong, but if an act is going to be perceived as wrong, then perhaps you shouldn't do it. But I only know that through retrospect." Bonin noted that people had "either forgotten the charges or come to the realization they amounted to nothing. A lot of them say I took an unfair beating. Of course the loyalists remain loyal and the critics I don't talk to."[580]

Bonin spoke about how difficult it was, in the months following his resignation, to resume his life as a Boston lawyer, going into court on behalf of a client, or encountering members of the judiciary or the bar in a restaurant or on a street corner. But he survived the ordeal. Summing up the experience, the former chief justice said, "No one dies of a broken heart."[581] In a letter after his resignation, he quoted from *The Book of Job:* "I hold fast my righteousness, and will not let it go; my heart does not reproach me for any of my days."[582]

A Brief History of the Bill of Address in Massachusetts

Removal by address has its origins in the British Act of Settlement of 1700, which provided among other things that upon the accession of the House of Hanover to the crown, judges would be appointed *quamdiu se bene gesserint*—literally, *depending on their good behavior*—"but upon the address of both Houses of Parliament it may be lawful to remove them."[583] Originally conceived as a method of assuring the independence of the judiciary—the sovereign could no longer remove a judge at will—the address quickly proved an unpopular removal device in England.[584] The last judge removed by a parliamentary address was Sir Jonah Barrington, in 1830.[585] In contrast, impeachment has only been used once to remove a Massachusetts judge—in 1821 against Middlesex Probate Judge James Prescott.[586] Address has been used with greater frequency.

Why has removal by address proven so durable in Massachusetts? Some answers may be found in the events leading up to the development of the Constitution of 1780.

As early as 1776, the farmers of Berkshire County had issued a petition declaring that

> since the Dissolution of the power of Great Britain over these colonies they have fallen into a state of Nature. That the first step to be taken by a people in such a state for the Enjoyment or Restoration of Civil government amongst them, is the formation of a fundamental Constitution as the basis and ground work of Legislation.[587]

An attempt to adopt a constitution in 1778 failed, but the effort only fueled the fire of those who insisted that there be a coherent form of government for the independent colony.

The Berkshire County Remonstrance of August 26, 1778, demanded the immediate call for a constitutional convention.[588] A new convention was called, and the first meeting was held in Cambridge on September 1, 1779. The convention turned to a committee of three—John Adams, Samuel Adams and the convention chairman, James Bowdoin—to draft a new frame of government. The drafting was delegated to John Adams, and it is largely his work that became the Massachusetts Constitution of 1780.[589]

Adams's inclusion of the address in the Constitution appears to have been an attempt to resolve nagging differences between the Berkshire farmers and the Boston merchants.[590] Rural farmers were dependent upon eastern merchants for goods and often fell into debt. It was frequently their experience that the courts were used primarily for debt collection purposes, and judges were viewed as servants of the eastern ruling class. Courts in Berkshire County were often closed as a demonstration of popular sovereignty.[591] Berkshire farmers and Boston merchants held common ground in their desire to have an independent judiciary, but the farmers also wanted some protection against life tenure judges who might oppress them. The address, which provided a method of removal by the elected representatives of the people, was likely familiar to Adams from his studies in the law, and judged by him as an effective compromise.[592]

Address was used on several occasions after adoption of the Constitution. Two judges (Whiting and Perry) were removed in 1787 for their conduct during Shays's rebellion (the "late, unhappy rebellion"), one judge (Bradbury) was removed in 1803 for infirmity, and two judges (Sargent and Vinal) were removed in 1803 after they were tried and convicted of extortion.[593]

Adams's son John Quincy, among other political leaders over the years, would express grave reservations about the wisdom and propriety of removal by address. The chief complaint was that, unlike impeachment, address offered no basic due process protections to the targeted judge. With no opportunity for an evidentiary hearing prior to removal, and with removal itself accomplished by simple majority vote, the address was viewed as a significant threat to judicial independence. John Quincy Adams, as a Massachusetts state senator, objected to the removal of Judges Sargent and Vinal by address, offering as reasons the threat to judicial independence if "the verdict of a jury in any one county of the Commonwealth" could be used to remove a judge with no further opportunity for hearing, and the failure of the address process to guarantee the judges "an opportunity previously to be heard in their own defense."[594]

In 1820, forty years after adoption of the Constitution, a convention was called for the purpose of improving the document. One element of debate was the address. Quincy Adams's view was shared by a majority of the men assembled in 1820—legal giants like Lemuel Shaw, Daniel Webster and Joseph Story. Daniel Webster rose to declare that removal by address was "against common right, as well as repugnant to the general principles of government ... To give an authority to the Legislature to deprive [a judge] of [his office], without trial or accusation, is manifestly to place judges at the pleasure of the Legislature. The question is not what the Legislature probably will do, but what they may do. If the judges, in fact, hold their offices only so long as the Legislature see fit, then it is vain and illusory to say that the judges are independent men, incapable of being influenced by hope or by fear; but the tenure of their office is not independent."[595]

A compromise was struck, and a proposed amendment to the Constitution was put before the people, providing that "no judicial officer shall be removed from office, until the alleged causes of removal are stated on the records of the Legislature; nor until the individual, thereby affected, shall have had an opportunity to be heard."[596] The amendment was offered to the people joined with two other proposed amendments, one providing for removal by address of justices of the peace and the other removing the ability of the governor and Legislature to ask advisory opinions of the Supreme Judicial Court.[597] The proposed amendments were defeated, with 14,518 nays against 12,471 yeas.

The Massachusetts Supreme Judicial Court has had only once occasion to opine on the constitutional propriety of removal by address. In 1883, Judge Joseph Day was removed for a number of offenses, including extortion, taking illegal fees, and public intoxication and rudeness. Day argued that in the absence of a judicial determination of his guilt, he could not be removed from office. The court reviewed the language of the Constitution and concluded that:

> When we consider the origin and history of the provision, the obvious and natural meaning of its language, and the uniform practical construction which has been given to it, we are forced to the conclusion that the intention of the people was to entrust the power of removal of a judicial officer to the two coordinate branches of government without limitation or restriction.

The court noted that the "Constitution authorizes the removal without any reason being assigned for it; and therefore it is wholly immaterial what evidence or causes induced the Legislature to vote the address, or led the governor and Council to act upon it."[598]

ACKNOWLEDGMENTS

I have many people to thank for helping me at various critical stages of this project. Suffolk University Professor Robert Allison was a mentor, friend and role model who nurtured my interest in writing history. His guidance and encouragement have provided me with the confidence to put pen to page. Harvard University Professor Stephan Thernstrom was a thoughtful and candid advisor when this book was in a much simpler form as a Master's Thesis. Professors Jim Goodman and the late William Gienapp provided the kind of inspiration and excitement that reinforced the idea that writing history is much more than an academic exercise.

The Supreme Judicial Court Clerk's office was enormously helpful in providing me with the tapes of the SJC trial, which I was able to copy and have transcribed. Larry Cameron was kind enough to help bring Garrett Byrne back to life for me, and provided me with material that proved very helpful in my understanding of the district attorney. Rudy Kikel provided me with a treasure trove of original copies of *Fag Rag*—sources that were instrumental to my understanding of the thinking underlying the Boston/Boise Committee. I am also indebted to each of the individuals who agreed to be interviewed for this book. It is a richer and more compelling work due in large part to their willingness to offer frank and uncensored comments about the events portrayed.

Robert and Angela Bonin were especially generous with their time. Their willingness to revisit a painful chapter in their lives, and to do so frequently and candidly, is something I will always be grateful for.

SOURCES

I knew or worked with several of the people identified in this book, including Robert Bonin, Francis Bellotti, Michael Dukakis and Francis Orfanello. Eleven people were interviewed for this book. The list below identifies these persons, the dates of the interviews, and the abbreviations used in the notes.

Mike Andersen—April 4, 2008: MA

Francis X. Bellotti—July 22, 2002: FXB

Angela Bonin—July 17, 1996: AB

Robert Bonin—February 9, 1996; February 15, 1996; March 1, 1996; July 11, 1996; July 31, 1996: RB

Robert and Angela Bonin—July 10, 1996: R/AB

Michael Dukakis—December 2, 1998: MSD

Thomas R. Kiley—December 14, 1998: TRK

Judge Dermot Meagher—July 24, 2002: DM

John Mitzel—July 1998: JM

Thomas Reeves—April 9, 1999: TCR

Harvey Silverglate—July 28, 2002: HS

Daniel Taylor—January 20, 2002: DAT

The Social Law Library has videotapes comprising oral histories of many individuals with relationships to law and politics in Boston. The oral history of Chief Justice Walter McLaughlin, recorded September 18, 1992, was particularly useful.

Copies of the Supreme Judicial Court tapes of the Bonin trial were provided to me by the SJC clerk's office. I had the tapes transcribed into nineteen volumes. The notes make reference to those volumes as "Transcript Vol."

Finally, Bob Bonin was generous in providing me with his personal papers from the period of his trial in 1978.

CITED WORKS

Books

Abramson, Jeffrey. *We the Jury: The Jury System and the Ideal of Democracy.* New York: Harper Collins, 1994.

Ainley, Leslie G. *Boston Mahatma: The Public Career of Martin M. Lomasney.* Boston: Bruce Humphries, 1949.

Amory, Cleveland. *The Proper Bostonians.* New York: Dutton, 1947.

Beatty, Jack. *The Rascal King.* Boston: Addison-Wesley, 1992.

Beebe, Lucius. *Boston and the Boston Legend.* New York: Appleton-Century, 1936.

Brooke, Edward. *Bridging the Divide: My Life.* New Brunswick: Rutgers Univ. Press, 2007.

Bulger, William. *While the Music Lasts.* Boston: Houghton Mifflin, 1996.

Burns, James McGregor. *The Vineyard of Liberty.* New York: Knopf, 1982.

Curley, James Michael. *I'd Do It Again: a Record of All My Uproarious Years.* Englewood Cliffs, NJ: Prentice Hall, 1957.

Curzon, L. B., ed. *English Legal History.* Plymouth (UK): Macdonald & Evans, 1979.

Cutler, John Henry. *Honey Fitz.* New York: Bobbs-Merrill, 1962.

Edelin, Kenneth C. *Broken Justice.* Martha's Vineyard, MA: PondView Press, 2008.

Foner, Eric. *Free Soil, Free Labor, Free Men.* London: Oxford Univ. Press, 1970.

Formisano, Ronald P. & Burns, Constance K., eds. *Boston 1700-1980: The Evolution of Urban Politics.* Westport, CT: Greenwood Press, 1984.

Fountain, Charles. *Another Man's Poison: The Life and Writing of Columnist George Frazier.* Chester, CT: Globe Pequot Press, 1984.

Gaines, Richard & Segal, Michael. *Dukakis: The Man Who Would Be President.* New York: Avon Books, 1987.

Garland, Joseph E. *Boston's North Shore.* Boston: Little, Brown & Co., 1978.

—. *Boston's Gold Coast: The North Shore, 1890-1929.* Boston: Little, Brown & Co., 1981.

Gerassi, John. *The Boys of Boise.* New York: Macmillan, 1966.

Goodwin, Doris Kearns. *The Fitzgeralds and the Kennedys.* New York: St. Martin's Press, 1988.

Handlin, Oscar. *Boston's Immigrants.* Boston: Athenaeum Press, 1972.

Hennessy, Michael E. *Massachusetts Politics: 1890-1935.* Norwood, MA: Norwood Press Linotype, 1935.

Hentoff, Nat. *Boston Boy.* New York: Knopf, 1986.

Kaiser, Charles. *The Gay Metropolis: 1940-1996.* Boston: Houghton Mifflin, 1997.

Kassin, Saul M. & Wrightsman, Lawrence S. *The American Jury on Trial: Psychological Perspectives.* New York: Hemisphere Publishing, 1988.

Kilgore, Kathleen. *John Volpe: The Life of an Immigrant's Son.* Dublin, NH: Yankee Books, 1987.

Levin, Murray B. *Kennedy Campaigning.* Boston: Beacon Press, 1966.

Loughery, John. *The Other Side of Silence: Men's Lives and Gay Identities—A Twentieth-Century History.* New York: Holt, 1998.

Lucas, J. Anthony. *Common Ground.* New York: Knopf, 1985.

Kenney, Charles and Turner, Robert. *Dukakis: An American Odyssey.* Boston: Houghton Mifflin, 1988.

Malone, Dumas, ed. *The Dictionary of American Biography, Vol. VI.* New York: Scribner, 1933.

Manchester, William. *A World Lit Only by Fire.* Boston: Little, Brown & Co., 1992.

McCauley, Peter E., II, *Revere Beach Chips: Historical Background from the Revere Journal.* Private Printing: Boston Public Library Collection, 1979.

Mitzel, John. *The Boston Sex Scandal.* Boston: Glad Day Books, 1980.

Moore, Patrick. *Beyond Shame: Reclaiming the Abandoned History of Radical Gay Sexuality.* Boston: Beacon Press, 2004.

Morris, James. *Heaven's Command: An Imperial Progress.* San Diego: Harcourt, Brace & Co., 1973.

Nazzaro, Edward & Frederick. *Revere Beach's Wonderland: Mystic City by the Sea.* Private Printing: Boston Public Library Collection, 1983.

Nixon, Richard M. *The Memoirs of Richard Nixon.* New York: Grosset & Dunlap, 1978.

O'Connor, Thomas H. *The Boston Irish: A Political History.* Boston: Northeastern Univ. Press, 1995.

—. *Building a New Boston: Politics and Urban Renewal 1950 to 1970.* Boston: Northeastern Univ. Press, 1993.

O'Toole, James M. *Militant and Triumphant: William Henry O'Connell and the Catholic Church in Boston.* Notre Dame: Univ. of Notre Dame Press, 1992.

Rechy, John. *The Sexual Outlaw.* New York: Grove Press, 1977.

Russell, Francis. *The Knave of Boston.* Boston: Quinlan Press, 1987.

Shand-Tucci, Douglas. *The Art of Scandal.* New York: Harper Collins, 1997.

—. *Boston Bohemia.* Amherst: Univ. of Massachusetts Press, 1995.

Southworth, Susan & Michael. *AIA Guide to Boston*. Chester, CT: Globe Pequot Press, 1992.

Starkey, Marion. *The Devil in Massachusetts*. New York: Knopf, 1949.

Stilgoe, John R. *Alongshore*. New London: Yale Univ. Press, 1994.

Trout, Charles H. *Boston: The Great Depression and the New Deal*. New York: Oxford Univ. Press, 1977.

Vidal, Gore. *Point to Point Navigation*. New York: Doubleday, 2006.

Wayman, Dorothy G. *David I. Walsh: Citizen Patriot*. Milwaukee: Bruce Publishing, 1952.

White, Theodore H. *In Search of History*. New York: Harper & Row, 1978.

Whitehill, Walter Muir. *Boston: A Topographical History*. Cambridge: Harvard Univ. Press, 1968.

Wolfe, Thomas. *Of Time and the River*. New York: Scribner, 1935.

United States Government Publications

Inaugural Addresses of the Presidents of the United States. Washington, DC: United States Government Printing Office, 1965.

The White House. Washington, DC: White House Historical Association, 1969.

Commonwealth of Massachusetts Government Publications

Bulletins for the Constitutional Convention, 1917-1918, Vol. 2. Boston: Wright & Potter (State Printer), 1919.

Public Document No. 43, Election Statistics, 1964 and 1978.

Comprehensive Report, Massachusetts Crime Commission, May 17, 1965.

Report on the State of the Massachusetts Court System. Governor's Select Committee on Judicial Needs, December 1976.

Public Document No. 144, Judicial Council of Massachusetts: 52d Report, 1976.

Public Document No. 144, Judicial Council of Massachusetts: 53rd Report, 1977.

Dalton, Cornelius, Wirkkala, John, & Thomas, Anne, eds. *Leading the Way: A History of the Massachusetts General Court: 1629-1980.* Boston: Secretary of the Commonwealth, 1984.

Journals, Reviews and Other Publications

Cella, Alexander. "The People of Massachusetts, the New Republic and the Constitution of 1780." *Suffolk Univ. Law Review* 14 (1980).

Comment. "Constitutional Processes for the Discipline of Judges in Massachusetts," *Boston College Annual Survey of Massachusetts Law* (1972).

Hennessey, Edward. "The Extraordinary Constitution of 1780." *Suffolk Univ. Law Review* 14 (1980).

Onello, Harriet Holzman. "The Massachusetts Bill of Address: Due Process Considerations of Judicial Removal." *Suffolk Univ. Law Review* 13 (1979).

Ray, Benjamin C. "Satan's War against the Covenant in Salem Village, 1692." *New England Quarterly* 80, no. 1 (March 2007).

Reported Judicial Decisions

Commonwealth v. Harriman, 134 Mass. 314 (1883).

Dennis v. United States, 341 U.S. 494, 525 (1951).

P.B.I.C., Inc. v. District Attorney of Suffolk County, 357 Mass. 763, 770-771 (1970).

P.B.I.C. Inc. v. Byrne, 313 F. Supp. 757, 765 (1970).

Byrne v. Karalexis, 401 U.S. 216 (1971).

In The Matter of Edward J. DeSaulnier, Jr., 360 Mass. 757 (1971).

In The Matter of Jerome Troy, 364 Mass. 15 (1973).

In The Matter of Francis X. Morrissey, 366 Mass. 11 (1974).

In The Matter of Francis J. Larkin, 368 Mass. 87 (1975).

Commonwealth v. Edelin, 371 Mass. 497 (1976).

Commonwealth v. Gilday, 474 Mass. 474, 491-492 (1975).

In The Matter of Robert M. Bonin, 375 Mass. 680, 695 (1978).

In The Matter of Orfanello, 411 Mass. 551 (1992).

PHOTO CREDITS

The author would like to thank the following individuals and organizations for their assistance in providing the photographs reprinted in this book. As film negatives were not available, digital scans of archived prints were provided to the publisher.

Aaron Schmidt of the Boston Public Library Print Department was helpful in providing the photographs donated to the BPL by predecessor newspaper companies to the present *Boston Herald,* which included the *Record American,* the *Sunday Advertiser,* the original *Boston Herald,* the *Boston Traveler,* the *Record American/Herald Traveler,* and the *Boston Herald American.*

Mike Andersen, former photographer for the *Boston Herald American,* was very accommodating in locating the photographs that he took of Robert and Angela Bonin at the Arlington Street Church on the night of April 5, 1978.

Alan Thibeault, Chief Librarian at the *Boston Herald,* kindly located the *Herald American* photograph of Frank Bellotti smoking a cigar after the swearing in of his new first assistant attorney general on March 8, 1977. This photograph was also taken by Mike Andersen.

Clif Garboden, Senior Managing Editor of the *Boston Phoenix,* generously supplied the photograph of Tom Reeves and John Mitzel. The photographer was not identified, however, the back caption read "June 5, 1978. Subject: Bonin Case—Suffolk Ct. House. Left to Right: John Mitzel, Sect. of Boston-Boise Committee & Dr. Tom Reeves Co-Chairman of Boston-Boise Committee."

- Figure 1: Francis X. Bellotti-unidentified photographer, March 15, 1972.
- Figure 2: Kevin White, Michael Dukakis and Edward Kennedy-photograph by Laban Whittaker, September 20, 1970.
- Figure 3: Michael Dukakis-photograph by Warren Patriquin, November 29, 1971.
- Figure 4: Walter McLaughlin, Sr. at a State House hearing in Gardner Auditorium-unidentified photographer, October 19, 1971.
- Figure 5: Garrett Byrne at the Parker House-photograph by Ulrike Welsch. September 16, 1970.
- Figure 6: Robert and Angela Bonin with Attorney General Francis Bellotti-photograph by Mike Andersen, March 8, 1977.
- Figure 7: Thomas Reeves and John Mitzel at the Suffolk County Courthouse during the Bonin trial-unidentified photographer, June 5, 1978.
- Figure 8: Robert and Angela Bonin at the Arlington Street Church-photograph by Mike Andersen, April 5, 1978.
- Figure 9: Gore Vidal and Robert Bonin-photograph by Mike Andersen, April 5, 1978.

ENDNOTES

1 *Boston Globe,* April 6, 1978; Transcript Vol. 12, 8. In his memoir *Point to Point Navigation,* Gore Vidal recalled "I was confronted with every speaker's nightmare. I had no written text; worse, no close knowledge of the events leading up to my appearance." Vidal, *Point to Point Navigation,* 222.

2 Transcript Vol. 13, 12.

3 *Boston Magazine,* Nancy Pomerene McMillan, "Angela!," July 1978, 140.

4 Transcript Vol. 18, 4.

5 Transcript Vol. 3, 13.

6 Vidal, *Point to Point Navigation,* 223.

7 *Inaugural Addresses of the Presidents,* 267.

8 *Boston Magazine,* Bo Burlingham, "Bellotti's Game," September 1981, 160; FXB interview.

9 FXB interview.

10 *Boston Business Journal,* John P. Driscoll, "Bellotti demurs about Duke's job," August 17, 1987, 20.

11 Only twice (for governor in 1970 and 1990) did Bellotti fail to win his party's nomination in a statewide election. He lost two general elections (for governor in 1964 and attorney general in 1966) and won four (lieutenant governor in 1962 and attorney general in 1974, 1978 and 1982).

12 *Boston Business Journal,* August 17, 1987, 20.

13 Ibid.

14 *Boston Evening Globe,* November 3, 1978, 2.

15 Bulger, *While the Music Lasts,* 205. Bellotti was in demand both as a lawyer and lecturer. His lectures were described as being "on an extremely high academic level and he has earned the respect of some of this country's outstanding professors of criminal law." Paul T. Smith, quoted in the *Boston Sunday Herald Advertiser,* July 28, 1974.

16 Nixon, *The Memoirs of Richard Nixon,* 265.

17 Lucas, *Common Ground,* 594.

18 FXB interview; author conversation with Kevin H. White.

19 FXB interview.

20 *Boston Business Journal,* August 17, 1987, 20.

21 FXB interview.

22 Gaines & Segal, *Dukakis,* 76.

23 Whitehill, *Boston in the Age of John Fitzgerald Kennedy,* 43; Bellotti defeated Peabody by 26,895 votes out of 751,000 cast. *Public Document No. 43, Election Statistics,* 217 (1964); Bellotti was viewed by many as the "upstart Italian American," Gaines & Segal, Dukakis, 76; *Boston Herald* columnist George Frazier referred to Bellotti as "the boy bocci player." Fountain, *Another Man's Poison,* 223.

24 Kilgore, *John Volpe,* 127-128.

25 *Public Document No. 43, Election Statistics,* 432 (1964). Bellotti lost the election by 23,046 votes out of 2.3 million cast.

26 Levin, *Kennedy Campaigning,* 106-107; Massachusetts Crime Commission.

27 Brooke, *Bridging the Divide,* 65.

28 Kenney & Turner, Dukakis: *An American Odyssey,* 61.

29 Gaines & Segal, *Dukakis,* 78.

30 Dukakis was bucking the system by running against the incumbent, Attorney General Robert Quinn. Dukakis was expected by Democratic Party regulars to run for the AG's seat, but he was determined to reach for the top prize. "That's the job I want," he told *Boston Globe* reporter Robert Turner. Turner e-mail to author, February 5, 2008.

31 *Boston Evening Globe,* November 6, 1974, 26.

32 *Boston Business Journal,* August 17, 1987, 20.

33 Brooke, *Bridging the Divide,* 141. Brooke recalls in his memoir that the "problem was that there was no clear evidence of abuse of the public trust... Elliot insisted that Bellotti had acted in an illegal fashion. I asked him to produce evidence, but he offered none. Since there was no plausible reason for Elliot to withhold such evidence, I had to conclude that he had none."

34 *Boston Globe,* Michael Kenney op-ed, October 1, 1974, 21.

35 FXB interview; *Boston Business Journal,* August 17, 1987, 20.

36 *Boston Globe,* Michael Kenney op-ed, October 1, 1974, 21.

37 Ibid.

38 *Boston Evening Globe,* October 30, 1974, 16 (Szep cartoon); *Boston Evening Globe,* November 6, 1974, 1.

39 *Boston Business Journal,* August 17, 1987, 20.

40 *Boston Evening Globe,* November 3, 1978, 2.

41 Ibid., November 6, 1974, 1.

42 Ibid., November 3, 1978, 2.

43 TRK interview.

44 *Boston Globe,* December 9, 1974, 10. Bellotti declared his first priority was to "reorganize the attorney general's office both physically and legally using the right kind of people."

45 *Boston Evening Globe* editorial, January 15, 1975, 3.

46 FXB interview.

47 *Boston Globe,* December 18, 1974, 3.

48 FXB interview.

49 *Boston Globe,* December 19, 1974, 37.

50 Even at the height of Dukakis's power as governor, in early 1988, the leaders of the old guard—predominantly Irish and Yankee politicians—openly attacked the governor in harsh terms. *Boston Globe,* March 5, 1988, B1 ("Thanks, and some memories. Passing political era reflected in fete for ex-Turnpike Chief Driscoll.")

51 Gaines & Segal, *Dukakis,* 169.

52 Kenney & Turner, *Dukakis: An American Odyssey,* 119.

53 Gaines & Segal, *Dukakis,* 174.

54 Kenney & Turner, *Dukakis: An American Odyssey,* 116-119.

55 Ibid., 201-202.

56 MSD interview.

57 *Governor's Select Committee on Judicial Needs,* 1.

58 Gaines & Segal, *Dukakis,* 202.

59 *Governor's Select Committee on Judicial Needs,* 4.

60 HS interview.

61 *Public Document No. 144, Judicial Council of Massachusetts: 53rd Report,* 1977, 8.

62 *Public Document No. 144, Judicial Council of Massachusetts: 52d Report,* 1976, 12.

63 *Boston Globe,* Francis G. Poitrast op-ed, "Court reform vs. the children," March 2, 1977, 16.

64 *Boston Globe,* January, 26, 1977, 7.

65 *Boston Evening Globe,* January 19, 1977, 10.

66 *Boston Globe,* David Farrell op-ed, "Cox panel key to Bonin flap," January 24, 1977, 14.

67 Brothers George and Charles were highly regarded trial lawyers, brother Richard the longtime state registrar of motor vehicles, sister Phyllis was chief clerk of the Cambridge Licensing Commission, brother Albert served as a senior executive with Lever Brothers. George was the first president of the Cambridge Civic Association. When scandal at the Metropolitan District Commission threatened to touch members of the State Senate, powerful Senate President John E. Powers called upon Walter and George McLaughlin to serve as special counsel to the body. The McLaughlin brothers undertook the task for no fee, and kept the investigators at bay.

68 HS interview; FXB interview.

69 FXB interview.

70 Walter McLaughlin Oral History, Social Law Library.

71 DM interview.

72 *Governor's Select Committee on Judicial Needs,* 4.

73 *Massachusetts Law Quarterly,* Spring 1977, 24.

74 *Boston Globe,* January 30, 1977, A6.

75 *Commonwealth v. Gilday.*

76 MSD interview.

77 *Governor's Select Committee on Judicial Needs,* 6.

78 *Boston Globe,* January 24, 1977, 14.

79 MSD interview.

80 HS interview.

81 *Boston Globe,* October 15, 1989, 29; 1978 political brochure, entitled "Mr. District Attorney," author's collection; *see also Boston Globe,* October 15, 1989, 29 quoting Byrne protégé Thomas Dwyer: "[Byrne] knew machine politics. He knew what people wanted. Frank Hogan, former Manhattan district attorney, and he were the two big district attorneys out of World War II. They were part of the public fascination with the concept of 'Mr. D.A.'"

82 *Boston Globe,* June 17, 1984, Focus Section, 1; Ibid., December 18, 1952, 19.

83 Ibid., June 17, 1984, Focus Section, 1.

84 Ibid., September 12, 1978, 3.

85 Ibid., June 17, 1984, Focus Section, 1.

86 O'Connor, *Building a New Boston,* 158.

87 Thomas Dwyer, a protégé of Byrne, once remarked "There is always something they say about the Irish. We never forget." *Boston Globe,* September 17, 1999, E1.

88 *Boston Evening Transcript,* September 3, 1924, 3.

89 Ibid., September 8, 1924, 3.

90 Amory, *Proper Bostonians,* 182.

91 *See generally,* Shand-Tucci, *The Art of Scandal.*

92 Malone, *Dictionary of American Biography,* 347-349.

93 Amory, *Proper Bostonians,* 72; O'Connor, *Boston Irish,* 156.

94 Hennessy, *Massachusetts Politics: 1890-1935,* 345.

95 Morris, *Heaven's Command,* 155; generally 152-167.

96 Lucas, *Common Ground,* 376-378; O'Toole, *Militant and Triumphant,* 83-86.

97 Beatty, *Rascal King,* 105; Trout, *Boston: Great Depression and New Deal,* 21-22.

98 Beatty, *Rascal King,* 105.

99 Goodwin, *Fitzgeralds and the Kennedys,* 186; *Boston Traveler,* December 2, 1935, 19.

100 Manchester, *A World Lit Only By Fire,* 10-11.

101 O'Toole, *Militant and Triumphant,* 242.

102 Ibid., 244.

103 Wolfe, *Of Time and the River,* 89 and 146.

104 *Boston Globe,* March 5, 1988, B1.

105 Ibid. ("Thanks, and some memories. Passing political era reflected in fete for ex-Turnpike Chief Driscoll.")

106 Conversation with Byrne on September 10, 1989, as recalled by Lawrence Cameron.

107 Ainley, *Boston Mahatma,* 3.

108 *Boston Globe,* September 7, 1924, 17.

109 Ibid., September 10, 1924, 13. No other candidate came close to Byrne, the next highest vote getter receiving 743 votes.

110 Charlestown was annexed by Boston in 1874.

111 Ibid., September 17, 1928, 1.

112 *Boston Traveler,* November 3, 1928, 1.

113 Chelsea, Revere and Winthrop are the three municipalities in Suffolk County that are not part of the City of Boston.

114 Beatty, *The Rascal King,* 337.

115 Ibid.

116 The *Boston Globe* referred to "Mayor Curley's whole hearted endorsement" of Foley. *Boston Globe,* October 20, 1933, 10. In his autobiography, Curley recalled: "I had backed Foley in 1933 when he ran" for mayor. Curley, *I'd Do It Again,* 299.

117 *Boston Globe,* November 5, 1933, 16.

118 Perhaps the best and most colorful evidence of this is the on-again, off-again relationship between Curley and Executive Councilor Daniel Coakley. They began as enemies in 1914, with Curley, in his first term as mayor, expressing pleasure that Coakley had resigned a city office, "relieving me of the task of removing him." Russell, *The Knave of Boston,* 3. The two men were such enemies over the years that in 1933 the *Boston Globe* thought it significant to report that they had shaken hands. *Boston Globe,* November 3, 1933.

119 *Boston Globe,* November 5, 1933, 16. The legendary ward boss of the West End, Martin Lomasney, was supporting Foley in a rare alliance with Curley. Unfortunately for Foley, Lomasney's best days were well behind him. Lomasney died in August of 1933. Ainley, *Boston Mahatma,* 238.

120 Curley, *I'd Do It Again,* 192; O'Connor, *The Boston Irish,* 198-199.

121 *Boston Globe,* November 7, 1933, 4.

122 Ibid.

123 Ibid., November 8, 1933, 1.

124 Nichols received 3,919 votes to Mansfield's 3,389 in Ward 12. Foley received 1,782 in a reflection of the citywide vote. *Boston Globe,* November 8, 1933, 14.

125 *Boston Globe,* November 8, 1933, 15.

126 *Boston Evening Globe,* December 1, 1952, 1; *Boston Herald,* December 2, 1952, 13.

127 *Boston Globe,* December 2, 1952, 20.

128 *Boston Evening Globe,* December 2, 1952, 1.

129 *Boston Herald,* December 2, 1952, 12.

130 Ibid.

131 Ibid., December 18, 1952, 26.

132 Ibid., December 18, 1952, 26. *The Herald's* long decline from the city's "newspaper of record" to the British-style, entertainment-oriented tabloid of the early 21st century is a sad story of the decline of the American newspaper.

133 *Boston Globe,* December 17, 1952, 1.

134 Ibid., 19.

135 Ibid., December 18, 1952, 18.

136 *Boston Herald,* December 18, 1952, 26.

137 *Boston Globe,* August 29, 1954, 1. O'Keefe escaped with only minor injuries from a "hail of machine gun bullets" aimed at him by Burke.

138 Ibid.

139 Ibid., 47.

140 *Boston Herald,* August 29, 1954, 1.

141 Ibid., August 30, 1954, 2. Presumably the *Herald* cleansed the precise quote to read "foul up" in order to maintain a family-friendly newspaper.

142 Ibid., September 7, 1954, 10.

143 Ibid., August 30, 1954, 2.

144 Ibid; *Boston Globe,* August 30, 1954, 3.

145 *Boston Herald,* September 5, 1954, 1.

146 Ibid., September 7, 1954, 1.

147 *Boston Evening Globe,* September 7, 1954, 1; *Boston Herald,* September 8, 1954,1; Ibid., September 9, 1954, 1.

148 *Boston Globe,* September 7, 1954, 3.

149 *Boston Herald,* September 5, 1954, 4.

150 *Boston Globe,* August 31, 1954, 1.

151 Ibid., September 1, 1954, 1.

152 Ibid., September 2, 1954, 16.

153 Ibid., September 11, 1954, 1.

154 *Boston Herald,* September 10, 1954, 16.

155 *Boston Globe,* September 13, 1954, 7.

156 *Boston Herald,* September 14, 1954, 1.

157 Ibid., August 29, 1954, 40.

158 *Boston Globe,* September 15, 1954, 20.

159 *New York Times,* May 11, 1965, 46.

160 Ibid.

161 Ibid.

162 *Boston Globe,* May 11, 1965, 49.

163 Ibid.

164 Ibid., May 9, 1965, 49.

165 Ibid., May 5, 1965, 1. "Byrne tries K.O. of Clay-Liston bout" said the page one *Boston Globe* headline.

166 Ibid., 53.

167 Ibid., May 6, 1965, 54.

168 Ibid.

169 Ibid., May 5, 1965, 53.

170 Ibid., May 8, 1965, 17.

171 Ibid., May 6, 1965, 1.

172 Ibid., 53.

173 Ibid., May 8, 1965, 4.

174 Ibid., May 6, 1965, 53.

175 Byrne's decision was a wise one since Inter-Continental never was licensed and the statutory obligation ran exclusively to the licensee.

176 *New York Times*, May 8, 1965, 25. The announcement of the change in venue highlighted the overwhelming importance of the ancillary rights to television, radio and motion picture revenues. The Boston Garden held 13,909, while the Lewiston Youth Center had a capacity of only 6,000. Clearly, the take from the gate was of little importance to the promoters. Ibid.

177 *Boston Globe*, May 7, 1965, 41.

178 Ibid., May 8, 1965, 17.

179 Ibid., May 11, 1965, 23.

180 Ibid.

181 Ibid.

182 Ibid., 49.

183 Ibid.

184 Ibid.

185 *New York Times,* July 27, 1965, 1.

186 *Boston Globe,* March 6, 1970, 16.

187 Beebe, *Boston and the Boston Legend,* 251-253.

188 *Boston Herald Traveler,* March 6, 1970, 20.

189 Ibid.

190 *P.B.I.C., Inc. v. District Attorney of Suffolk County.* Describing the play as a "noisy, disorganized performance," the Court noted that *Hair* "constitutes, in some degree, an obscure form of protest protected by the First Amendment."

191 *Boston Globe,* March 2, 1970, 10.

192 *P.B.I.C. Inc. v. Byrne.*

193 In an editorial, the *Boston Globe* advised that "closing down the show would both defeat its own purpose and lose, not gain, political support for whoever ordered it done." *Boston Globe,* March 2, 1970, 10.

194 *Byrne v. Karalexis.*

195 Edelin, *Broken Justice,* 3, 18.

196 *Boston Globe,* February 16, 1975, 2; February 19, 1975, 1-3.

197 Ibid., January 12, 1975, 34; January 13, 1975, 5.

198 Ibid., February 16, 1975, 5.

199 Edelin, *Broken Justice,* 82.

200 Ibid., 76.

201 *Boston Globe,* January 17, 1975, 1-10; February 4, 1975, 1; February 6, 1975, 1; February 16, 1975, 1-14, *Commonwealth v. Kenneth Edelin.*

202 *Boston Globe,* January 11, 1975, 1.

203 *Boston Globe,* February 9, 1977, 33; *Massachusetts Lawyers Weekly,* June 16, 1997, 11.

204 Edelin, *Broken Justice,* 101.

205 *Boston Globe,* January 11, 1975, 3; January 12, 1975, 29-34.

206 Ibid., February 16, 1975, 5.

207 Ibid.

208 *New York Times,* February 14, 1975, 36.

209 Ibid.

210 *Boston Globe,* February 18, 1975, 1. Eventually, his conviction was overturned on appeal. *Commonwealth v. Edelin.*

211 Edelin, *Broken Justice,* 342.

212 Ibid., 341.

213 *New York Times,* February 19, 1975, 34.

214 *Boston Globe,* February 19, 1975, 22.

215 Ibid., 3.

216 *Commonwealth v. Edelin.*

217 *Boston Globe,* September 12, 1978, 3.

218 *Public Document No. 43, Election Statistics,* 331 (1974). Byrne won with 47,734 votes. His opponents collectively garnered 56,037 votes, and 25,318 voters left their ballots blank.

219 *Boston Globe,* September 12, 1978, 18.

220 Ibid., 3.

221 Ibid., September 17, 1978, 19.

222 Mitzel, *The Boston Sex Scandal,* 28.

223 Garland, *Boston's North Shore.* For his book, Garland reproduced an 1880s "Point of Pines" poster from the Boston Public Library Print Department collection.

224 McCauley, *Revere Beach Chips*. The great charm of the place was captured by a poem that appeared in the *Revere Journal,* August 27, 1887:

> Thousands stood to hear the music,
> Piccolo, trombone, cornet fine.
> And the hundreds more were hearing
> While they sat in halls to dine.
>
> From piazza 'twas a study
> Just to watch the changing crowds
> And the faces pale or ruddy,
> Forms erect or bent and bowed.
> On Revere's old shore of ocean
> Thousands have this summer roamed,
> Gazed beyond at mighty waters,
> Watched the waves that dashed and foamed.

225 *The White House,* 78.

226 *See generally,* Garland, *Boston's Gold Coast,* 20-21; Nazzaro, *Revere Beach's Wonderland.*

227 *See generally,* Nazzaro, *Revere Beach's Wonderland;* McCauley, *Revere Beach Chips.*

228 Ibid.

229 Garland, *Boston's North Shore,* 22.

230 McCauley, *Revere Beach Chips.*

231 *Village Voice,* Frank Rose, "Men & Boys Together," February 23, 1978, 17.

232 Ibid., 17.

233 Mitzel, *The Boston Sex Scandal*, 20; *Village Voice*, 14.

234 *Village Voice*, February 23, 1978, 17.

235 RB interview, February 15, 1996.

236 R/AB interview, July 10, 1996.

237 RB interview, February 15, 1996.

238 *Boston Globe*, December 23, 1974, 3. Bonin told the *Boston Globe* that "Frank has assured me that the chain of command will be from me to him, not around me." Ibid.

239 FXB interview.

240 White, *In Search of History*, 14. For many young Jewish boys like White, the Irish were "then the established menace"; Hentoff, *Boston Boy*, 28-31. Bonin experienced some antagonism from neighboring Irish youth, and would hear the occasional references to the main street in his Blue Hill Avenue neighborhood as "Jew Hill Avenue," but in looking back on these times he did not recall much direct experience with anti-Semitism. "The worst might be some fighting or a bloody nose," he recalled, "but I wouldn't overstate it. It wasn't a major factor in my growing up." RB interview, February 9, 1996.

241 O'Connor, *The Boston Irish*, 239-240.

242 Hentoff, *Boston Boy*, 37.

243 AB interview, July 17, 1996.

244 R/AB interview, July 10, 1996.

245 Ibid.

246 Ibid.

247 Ibid.

248 Ibid.

249 TRK interview.

250 *Boston Magazine,* 113, 164-165; *Boston Globe* State House columnist Carol Surkin wrote that "Bellotti, after three years as attorney general, ranks with the state's most popular politicians." *Boston Sunday Globe,* October 2, 1977, A6.

251 TRK interview.

252 *Boston Globe,* March 8, 1977, 7.

253 Bonin remarks to author, Summer 1976.

254 *Boston Globe,* December 23, 1974, 3.

255 RB interview, February 9, 1996.

256 *Boston Globe,* David Farrell op-ed, "Cox panel key to Bonin flap," January 24, 1977, 14.

257 DAT interview.

258 MSD interview.

259 TRK interview.

260 Governor Charles F. Hurley appointed former Congressman John P. Higgins to the post in 1937; Governor Christian Herter selected his legal counsel, Paul Reardon, as Superior Court chief justice in 1955. *Boston Globe,* January 19, 1977, 10.

261 Ibid., January 31, 1977, 1.

262 R/AB interview, July 10, 1996.

263 *Boston Globe,* January 20, 1977, 1.

264 Ibid., January 19, 1977, 10; Ibid., January 20, 1977, 15.

265 Richard McLaughlin was returned to his post as the Commonwealth's Registrar of Motor Vehicles by Governor Edward King, who defeated Dukakis in the 1978 Democratic primary. McLaughlin became briefly controversial by establishing the requirement that Registry officials refer to themselves with military sobriquets. Richard McLaughlin was, of course, "the General." In 1983 he was again replaced by Dukakis, who had returned to office after a "rematch" with King.

266 MSD interview.

267 *The Real Paper,* Harvey Silverglate, "Knowing Bonin by his enemies," April 1978, 12.

268 *Boston Evening Globe,* "Bonin and the real issue," March 2, 1977, 16.

269 McLaughlin Oral History.

270 *Boston Globe,* January 21, 1977, 15.

271 Ibid., 7.

272 Ibid., March 3, 1977, 8.

273 MSD interview.

274 *Boston Globe,* David Farrell op-ed, "Cox panel key to Bonin flap," January 24, 1977, 14.

275 Ibid., January 26, 1977, 7.

276 RB interview, March 1, 1996.

277 Lucas, *Common Ground,* 495.

278 Comments by Alfred S. Larkin Jr., Boston Globe VP and Assistant to the Publisher, *Boston Globe* July 27, 1998, B9.

279 HS interview.

280 *Boston Globe,* January 19, 1977, 10.

281 Ibid., February 20, 1977, 1.

282 Ibid., February 21, 1977, 34.

283 The *Boston Globe* noted that the position of Superior Court chief justice "is one of the most important jobs in the state and if the Cox Committee recommendations for reorganizing the court system go through, it will carry with it even greater responsibilities than it does now." *Boston Globe* editorial, February 25, 1977, 22.

284 *Boston Globe,* March 2, 1977, 1.

285 DM interview.

286 WBZ editorial, February 3, 1977.

287 *Boston Globe* editorial, February 25, 1977, 22.

288 MSD interview.

289 *Boston Globe,* February 1, 1977.

290 Ibid., March 3, 1977, 3.

291 MA interview. Andersen twice was awarded the distinction of taking the "New England Press Photo of the Year." He would figure significantly in Bonin's future. Bellotti's victory cigar was a custom he shared with his close personal friend, Celtics Coach "Red" Auerbach.

292 Thomas Winship, letter to Robert Bonin, March 4, 1977, Bonin papers.

293 *Boston Herald American,* March 8, 1977, 1.

294 *Boston Evening Globe,* March 8, 1977, 7.

295 RB interview, March 1, 1996.

296 FXB interview.

297 HS interview.

298 *Boston Magazine,* July 1978, 61. At the time of Bonin's appointment, the chief justices of the District Court, Probate Court and Boston Municipal Court were Jewish. Nancy Pomerene McMillan reported that the *Globe's* Joe Harvey's "disaffection with Bonin was no secret—his

reports, for instance, were sprinkled with references to Bonin's Jewishness." Prominent criminal defense attorney Harvey Silverglate wrote that "some critics were reported—all anonymously, of course—to be unhappy with the elevation of a Jew as chief justice of the Superior Court." *The Real Paper,* April 1978.

299 R/AB interview, July 10, 1996.

300 RB interview, July 11, 1996.

301 *Boston Magazine,* July 1978, 61.

302 *Massachusetts Lawyer's Weekly,* April 11, 1977, 6.

303 *Boston Herald American,* March 13, 1977, 7.

304 *Boston Globe,* April 24, 1977, 1.

305 Ibid., 6.

306 RB interview, July 11, 1996.

307 HS interview.

308 *The Real Paper,* April 1978, 12.

309 RB interview, July 11, 1996.

310 Ibid.

311 *The Real Paper,* April 1978, 12.

312 Ibid.

313 RB interview, July 11, 1996.

314 Ibid.

315 *Boston Magazine,* July 1978, 61.

316 *The Boston Phoenix,* Richard Gaines, "The self-sabotage of Robert Bonin," April 25, 1978, 28.

317 RB interview, July 11, 1996.

318 *Boston Magazine,* July 1978.

319 *Boston Sunday Globe,* April 16, 1978, 12.

320 *Boston Magazine,* July 1978, 60.

321 AB interview, July 17, 1996.

322 R/AB interview, July 10, 1996.

323 *Boston Globe,* February 25, 1977, 22.

324 DM interview.

325 AB interview, July 17, 1996.

326 DM interview.

327 *Comment,* Boston University Law School, April 5, 1977, 1.

328 AB interview, July 17, 1996.

329 Ibid.

330 Ibid.

331 Supreme Judicial Court Rule 3:25, Canon 5C(4)(c).

332 Transcript Vol. 2, 24.

333 Ibid.

334 Ibid.; AB interview, July 17, 1996.

335 DAT interview.

336 MSD interview.

337 *Boston Globe,* December 1, 1977, 27.

338 Robert M. Bonin, letter to Allan Rodgers, November 30, 1977, Bonin papers.

339 *Boston Herald American,* December 4, 1977, 1.

340 Ibid.; *Boston Globe,* December 11, 1977, 1.

341 *Boston Herald American,* December 7, 1977: 1.

342 *Boston Globe,* December 7, 1977, 1.

343 Ibid., December 6, 1977, 22.

344 *Boston Herald American,* December 2, 1977, 1.

345 DAT interview.

346 *Boston Globe,* December 7, 1977, 8.

347 *Boston Sunday Globe,* April 16, 1978, 12.

348 AB interview, July 17, 1996.

349 *Boston Globe,* December 13, 1977, 1.

350 MSD interview.

351 *Boston Globe,* December 4, 1977, 4.

352 Frank Bellotti was Farrell's "close friend and handball partner" since the early 1960s. Fountain, *Another Man's Poison,* 223.

353 *Boston Globe,* December 9, 1977, 19.

354 *Massachusetts Lawyer's Weekly,* October 16, 1995, 11.

355 *Boston Globe,* December 9, 1977, 10.

356 *Village Voice,* February 23, 1978, 17. In Massachusetts any sex act with a minor (a person under 16 years of age) is rape, without regard to consent.

357 Mitzel, *Boston Sex Scandal,* 44.

358 *Village Voice,* February 23, 1978, 20.

359 Mitzel, *Boston Sex Scandal,* 44.

360 *Boston Globe,* December 9, 1977, 17.

361 *Village Voice,* February 23, 1978, 1.

362 Mitzel, *Boston Sex Scandal,* 27.

363 Ibid., 32.

364 *Boston Evening Globe,* December 9, 1977, 15.

365 *Boston Globe,* December 10, 1977, 3.

366 HS interview.

367 *Boston Traveler,* December 15, 1935, 1.

368 Wayman, *David I. Walsh: Citizen Patriot,* 43.

369 Gore Vidal, in an interview with the publication *Fag Rag,* claimed that Walsh "tried to make my father when my father was a West Point cadet. Chased my father and his roommate … and Senator Walsh picked them up. They were both very innocent West Pointers. My father said it was just appalling." Gore Vidal interview, *Fag Rag #7/8,* Winter/Spring 1974, 1.

370 Wayman, *David I. Walsh,* 309-319. Walsh received just over one million votes when he won re-election to the Senate in 1940. In 1946, running against Henry Cabot Lodge, Jr., Walsh's vote plummeted to 660,200. Many factors—his age, Lodge's stature—no doubt explain the reason for Walsh's defeat. But the taint of homosexuality no doubt contributed mightily to his lopsided defeat.

371 Loughery, *The Other Side of Silence,* 207.

372 *Fag Rag,* Shannon Austin, "The Pink Scare," 1979, 3.

373 Ibid., unsigned editorial, Fall 1978, 1.

374 Ibid., June/July 1976, 2.

375 Ibid., Thomas Reeves, "Faggots, Terror and the Law," *Fag Rag* Fall Supplement, 1978, 6; *Fag Rag,* Issue #26, 1.

376 Moore, *Beyond Shame,* 7.

377 *Fag Rag,* Charles Shively, "Cocksucking as an Act of Revolution," Issue#3, Summer 1972, 8.

378 Ibid., Shively, "Pure Sex," *Issue #41.*

379 Ibid., Shively, "To Speak the Unspeakable," Fall Supplement, 1978, 9.

380 Ibid., Issue *#20,* 15.

381 Ibid., 14.

382 JM interview.

383 *Fag Rag,* Thomas Reeves, Fall 1978, 4. The self description as sexual outlaws was a reference to John Rechy's book, *The Sexual Outlaw,* which had been published in 1977, and which extolled "promiscuous homosexuals (outlaws with dual identities—tomorrow they will go to offices and athletic fields, classrooms and construction sites) [who] are the shock troops of the sexual revolution." Rechy explained that to be a sexual outlaw, one must be an "archetypical outsider, a symbol of survival, living fully at the edge, triumphant over the threats, repression, persecution, prosecution, attacks, denunciations, hatred that have tried powerfully to crush him from the beginning of 'civilization' ... [the

outlaw is] only a tiny segment of the vast homosexual world—secretly admired and envied but publicly put down by the majority of safe homosexuals cozy in heterosexual imitation..." John Rechy, *The Sexual Outlaw*, 299.

384 *Village Voice*, February 27, 1978, 18.

385 *Fag Rag*, unsigned editorial, "What is is what needs to be destroyed," Issue #26, 1.

386 TCR interview.

387 JM interview.

388 TCR interview.

389 *Fag Rag*, "Of Boys and Baltimore," Feb/March 1978, 3.

390 Ibid.

391 In a 1999 interview, Reeves went out of his way to point out that neither Shively nor Mitzel were pederasts. Their support for intergenerational sex arose as a part of their overall views toward sexual freedom, and rebellion against perceived heterosexual norms, not from personal predilection. TCR interview; Mitzel, *Boston Sex Scandal*, 134-135.

392 The emotions generated by the hotline were exacerbated by the decidedly anti-gay tenor of the times. Mitzel opined in his book, *The Boston Sex Scandal*, that "Gay liberation became, in the late '70s, the most significant and threatening social movement in the U.S." Ibid.

Through the spring and early summer of 1977, much attention had been lavished on Anita Bryant's crusade to repeal a gay rights ordinance in Dade County, Florida. Bryant, the popular spokesperson for the Florida Citrus Growers Commission and a former Miss Oklahoma, brought a religious fervor to her effort to rescind an ordinance that did nothing more than ban discrimination based upon "affectional or sexual preference." Her campaign to repeal the ordinance became a moral battleground, focused not on the merits of the law but on fears engendered by negative stereotypes of gay males. Naming her effort a campaign to "Save Our Children," Bryant minced no words about her concern that since homosexuals "cannot reproduce, they must recruit." Bryant's appeal was enormously effective, and Dade County voters repealed the ordinance by a vote of 202,319 to 89,562. Ibid.

It was a stunning defeat for the gay rights movement, and it left the opponents of equal rights for gays and lesbians emboldened to pursue similar initiatives in other venues. Successful efforts to repeal equal rights ordinances took place after ugly campaigns in St. Paul, Minnesota, Wichita, Kansas and Eugene, Oregon.

393 Mitzel, *Boston Sex Scandal,* 34.

394 Ibid.

395 Gerassi, *The Boys of Boise,* 30-31. In Boise, the arrest of two men on morals charges led to unsubstantiated charges by local prosecutors of the existence of a wide homosexual sex ring. A virtual panic ensued, resulting in the questioning of nearly fifteen hundred citizens, and the arrest and incarceration of nearly a dozen men, many for the "crime" of having consensual sex with other adult men.

396 *Village Voice,* February 27, 1978, 18.

397 Ibid.

398 Ibid., *Boston Sex Scandal,* 48.

399 Ibid.

400 TCR interview.

401 *Village Voice,* February 27, 1978, 19.

402 Mitzel, *Boston Sex Scandal,* 53.

403 JM interview; TCR interview.

404 *Fag Rag,* Emergency Supplement, February/March 1978, 1.

405 Mitzel, *Boston Sex Scandal,* 30.

406 *Village Voice,* February 27, 1978, 17; *Fag Rag,* February/March 1978.

407 *Fag Rag,* Double Issue #23/24, Fall 1978. Ginsberg had his poetic facts wrong—Byrne was not a bachelor.

408 *Village Voice,* February 27, 1978, 17.

409 Ibid.

410 Thomas Reeves, letter to defense counsel, February 16, 1978. Bonin papers.

411 Kassin & Wrightsman, *The American Jury on Trial*, 57-58; Abramson, *We The Jury*, 148-155.

412 Transcript Vol. 4, 4.

413 Ibid.

414 TCR interview.

415 Transcript Vol. 4, 8-9.

416 *In the Matter of Robert M. Bonin*, 697.

417 DM interview.

418 Transcript Vol. 12, 8.

419 Ibid.

420 Ibid., 6.

421 Ibid., 4.

422 Ibid., 8.

423 Transcript Vol. 13, 12.

424 Transcript Vol. 12, 10.

425 Ibid., 11-14.

426 RB interview, July 31, 1996.

427 Transcript Vol. 18, 4.

428 RB interview, July 31, 1996.

429 *Boston Globe,* December 23, 1982, 2.

430 *Boston Herald American,* April 6, 1978, 1+.

431 *Boston Evening Globe,* April 6, 1978, 1.

432 TCR interview.

433 MA interview.

434 MA interview.

435 *The Herald American* was assured of scooping the *Globe* because the Bonin story did not make the paper's first edition. As explained by Mike Andersen, the two city newspapers would review each other's first editions, and if there was a story of note, they had some time to play catch up. But if a story only made it to the final edition, it was too late for the competitor newspaper to do anything about it. MA interview.

436 *Boston Magazine,* July 1978, 62.

437 FXB interview.

438 TCR interview.

439 AB interview, July 17, 1996.

440 *Boston Globe,* April 7, 1978, 1; *Boston Herald American,* April 7, 1978, 1+.

441 Walter McLaughlin, letter to members of the Massachusetts Bar, April 3, 1978. Bonin papers.

442 Mitzel, *Boston Sex Scandal,* 13; Political advertisement from author's collection.

443 *Boston Evening Globe,* April 7, 1978, 1+.

444 *Boston Globe,* April 8, 1978, 1

445 Ibid., 2.

446 Ibid., 8.

447 *Quincy Patriot Ledger,* April 8, 1978.

448 *Boston Herald American,* April 8, 1978, 2.

449 TCR interview.

450 Thomas Reeves, letter to Robert Bonin, April 9, 1978. Bonin papers.

451 Transcript Vol. 10, 24.

452 *Boston Globe,* April 10, 1978, 16.

453 Vidal, *Point to Point Navigation,* 223.

454 *Boston Evening Globe,* April 6, 1978, 1.

455 *Boston Globe,* April 11, 1978, 1; *Boston Herald American,* April 11, 1978, 1.

456 *Boston Evening Globe,* April 11, 1978, 20. Angela Bonin publicly questioned whether "McLaughlin has put Chief Justice Hennessey in a difficult position where the public might question his own impartiality." *Boston Globe,* April 18, 1978, 8.

457 *Boston Herald American,* April 11, 1978, 1.

458 Ibid., 1; *Boston Evening Globe,* April 10, 1978, 1.

459 *Boston Herald American,* April 11, 1978, 1.

460 *In the Matter of Jerome Troy,* 15.

461 *Boston Globe,* April 29, 1978, 1+.

462 Robert Bonin, letter to Michael Dukakis. April 11, 1978. Bonin papers.

463 *Boston Globe,* April 12, 1978, 1.

464 Robert Bonin, letter to Edward Hennessey, April 12, 1978. Bonin papers.

465 Supreme Judicial Court, notice to Robert M. Bonin, April 12, 1998. Bonin papers.

466 *Boston Evening Globe,* April 12, 1978, 1.

467 Ibid., 1.

468 John Ward, letter to Robert Bonin, April 13, 1978. Bonin papers.

469 Thomas Reeves, letter to Angela and Robert Bonin, August 8, 1978. Bonin papers.

470 *Boston Globe,* April 13, 1978, 1+.

471 Vidal, *Point to Point Navigation,* 223.

472 *Boston Globe,* April 13, 1978, 1+.

473 Ibid.

474 Ibid., 14. Angela Bonin would recall: "I understand that Paul Sugarman is a brilliant attorney. I don't think he did a brilliant job with my husband." AB interview, July 17, 1996.

475 *Boston Globe,* Ken Hartnett, "Will the facts support the appearances in the Bonin case?" April 15, 1978, 7.

476 *Boston Herald American,* April 14, 1978, 1, 6.

477 Ray, "Satan's War against the Covenant in Salem Village," 91.

478 Vincent A. DiGangi, letter to Robert M. Bonin, July 9, 1978. Bonin papers.

479 Beverly Varlman, postcard to Angela and Robert Bonin, July 27, 1978. Bonin papers.

480 William E. Halliday, letter to Robert M. Bonin, July 20, 1978. Bonin papers.

481 Mr. & Mrs. Sam Wigowsky, letter to Robert M. Bonin. July 2,

1978. Bonin papers.

482 Anonymous, letter to Robert M. Bonin, September 5, 1978.
Bonin papers.

483 Brian Carr, letter to Robert M. Bonin, July 20, 1978. Bonin
papers.

484 *Boston Herald American,* April 15, 1978, 1+.

485 Joseph G. Tauro, draft letter to Paul Sugarman and David Sargent,
May 24, 1978. Bonin papers.

486 Ibid.

487 AB interview, July 17, 1996. Angela may have also been upset by
a letter sent by Sugarman and Sargent to *Boston Magazine,* defending
Boston Globe court reporter Joseph Harvey in glowing terms as a
"conscientious, able and highly-principled reporter." Sugarman and
Sargent Letter to Editor, *Boston Magazine,* August 16, 1978. Bonin
papers. Given Harvey's shabby treatment of Bonin from the very
beginning — a treatment that even *Globe* editor Thomas Winship took
issue with — the Sugarman/Sargent letter must have been particularly
galling and unfathomable to Angela.

488 AB interview, July 17, 1996.

489 RB interview, July 31, 1996.

490 AB interview, July 17, 1996.

491 Francis Masuret, handwritten account, April 11, 1978. Bonin papers.

492 *In the Matter of Robert M. Bonin,* 698.

493 Transcript, Vol. 6, 19-20.

494 Transcript Vol. 16, 15.

495 Ibid., 14 and 15.

496 *Boston Herald American,* April 8, 1978, 2.

497 Transcript Vol. 16, 15.

498 Starkey, *The Devil in Massachusetts,* 28.

499 John Ward, letter to Robert Bonin, April 13, 1978. Bonin papers.

500 Transcript Vol. 13, 7-8.

501 TCR interview. For his part, Bonin never grasped what Reeves was saying. "It sounds stupid to say I was not being attentive to his remarks, but I certainly didn't go to the lecture to hear Tom Reeves," recalled Bonin in an interview. RB interview, July 31, 1996.

502 Transcript Vol. 4, 24.

503 Ibid., 18.

504 Reeves never had trouble making the distinction. In a *Globe* editorial opinion piece, he wrote "We did not raise funds for the defendants… There is an important distinction between work to assure fair trials and work to defend individuals. Our work and the statements at the meeting are in line with civil liberties work, not defense." *Boston Globe,* April 17, 1978, 19.

505 Transcript Vol. 5, 4.

506 Ibid., 5.

507 Superior Court Judge John Meagher recalled Orfanello telling him that he spoke with Bonin only for a few seconds. Transcript Vol. 10, 14.

508 Transcript Vol. 2, 36.

509 Ibid., 37. Bonin would later admit to hearing "polemics expressed against the district attorney's office" while seated in the church. "One could say that when they were voiced I should have gotten up and walked out. I considered that, but then, I don't know, maybe it was stubbornness, I felt the best thing to do would be to stay and listen gracefully." *Boston Globe,* December 23, 1982, 2. The question before the Supreme Judicial Court in 1978 was, of course, not whether Bonin had heard polemics against District Attorney Byrne at the Arlington Street Church, but whether Bonin knew prior to attending the lecture that it was a fund raiser for the Revere defendants.

510 Transcript Vol. 16, 11.

511 Ibid., 16.

512 Ibid., 17.

513 Transcript Vol. 6, 15.

514 Ibid., 18.

515 Ibid.

516 Transcript Vol. 8, 42.

517 Ibid., 32; Transcript Vol. 7, 13. Orfanello's actual note had errors in spelling (he misspelled "Brian" as "Bryan" and he misspelled "Committee") not reflected in the text.

518 Transcript Vol. 6, 8.

519 Transcript Vol. 7, 14-19.

520 Transcript Vol.6, 11.

521 Ibid., 13.

522 Ibid., 14.

523 MA interview.

524 Transcript Vol. 7, 45.

525 Transcript Vol. 17, 13-14.

526 Ibid., 5.

527 Ibid., 14 and Vol. 16, 10.

528 Transcript Vol. 17, 14.

529 *Dennis v. United States,* 525 (Justice Frankfurter, concurring).

530 Amicus Brief filed by the Civil Liberties Union of Massachusetts, *In the Matter of Robert Bonin,* SJC docket 78-152-CIV.

531 *In the Matter of Robert M. Bonin,* 695.

532 Ibid., 696.

533 Ibid., 705.

534 Ibid.

535 Ibid.

536 Ibid., 706.

537 Ibid.

538 Ibid., 706, 707.

539 Ibid., 708.

540 Ibid., 729.

541 Ibid.

542 Ibid., 711, 712.

543 *In the Matter of Edward J. DeSaulnier, Jr.,* 757.

544 *In the Matter of Jerome P. Troy,* 15.

545 *In the Matter of Francis J. Larkin,* 87.

546 *In the Matter of Francis X. Morrissey,* 11.

547 WEEI editorial, "Bonin Part 2," August 8, 1978.

548 Onello, "The Massachusetts Bill of Address: Due Process Considerations of Judicial Removal," 1319, 1334, n. 79.

549   Ibid at note 81. *See also* Mass. H.R. Doc. No. 107 (1858)
(Minority Report in the Loring Matter).

550   Joel Brauser, letter to Robert Bonin, July 25, 1978. Bonin papers.

551   WBZ editorial, "The Bonin Case," July 14, 1978.

552   *Boston Globe,* David Farrell, "Dukakis the target of flap over
Bonin," January 27, 1977, 25.

553   *Boston Globe,* August 22, 1982, 1.

554   MSD interview.

555   *Massachusetts House Journal,* July 31, 1978.

556   Robert M. Bonin, press statement of July 20, 1978. Bonin papers.

557   *Boston Globe,* July 25, 1978, 1.

558   *Massachusetts House Journal,* July 31, 1978, 6-10.

559   Ibid., 10-11.

560   Ibid. Among the seventeen House members voting not to remove
Bonin were Charles Flaherty, later to be house speaker, and Paul
Cellucci, later to be governor of the Commonwealth.

561   *Massachusetts Senate Journal,* July 31, 1978, 9.

562   MSD interview.

563   Robert M. Bonin, letter to Michael Dukakis, August 2, 1978.
Bonin papers.

564   Michael Dukakis, letter to Robert M. Bonin, August 2, 1978. Bonin papers.

565   Bonin papers. *See also* Onello, "The Massachusetts Bill of Address," 1342, n. 141.

566   Vidal, *Point to Point Navigation,* 223.

567   Gore Vidal, letter to Robert M. Bonin, postmarked from Ravello, Italy, August 14, 1978. Bonin papers.

568   AB interview, July 17, 1996.

569   *Boston Magazine,* Nancy Pomerene McMillan, "Angela!," July 1978, 142.

570   AB interview, July 17, 1996.

571   St. 1978, chapter 478.

572   A more substantial court reform bill was enacted into law in 1992. The 1992 law created an office of chief justice for administration and management of the trial court, who is appointed "from among the justices of the trial court departments, by a majority of the justices of the supreme judicial court." St. 1992, chapter 379, section 73. The chief justices of the various trial courts were also chosen from among the sitting justices. Thus future efforts at court reform ensured that the Dukakis model of appointing a chief justice from outside the system would never recur.

573   Ibid., Section 1.

574 Flanagan defeated Byrne by a little over ten thousand votes,
42,888 to 32,037. Byrne lost every city and town in Suffolk County
except Chelsea. *Public Document No. 43, Election Statistics,* 189 (1978).

575 JM interview.

576 Lawrence Cameron, remarks on the occasion of the dedication of
a bust of Garrett Byrne at Suffolk University Law School, April 1991.
Cameron papers.

577 Mayor Kevin White and District Attorney Newman Flanagan led
the procession at the funeral. Dwyer, Thomas memorandum re: Byrne
Funeral Seating, October 14, 1989. Cameron papers.

578 *In the Matter of Orfanello,* 551.

579 RB interview, February 16, 1996.

580 *Boston Globe,* December 23, 1982, 21.

581 Ibid., 2.

582 Robert Bonin, letter to Thomas Reeves, quoting the *Book of Job*
27:2-6, August 11, 1978.

583 Curzon, *English Legal History,* 210.

584 Onello, "The Massachusetts Bill of Address," 1321-22, n. 11.
("The victory of the Act of settlement was its limitation on royal
arbitrariness rather than its enhancement of the power of Parliament
over judges.") In an address proceeding in 1806, the House of Lords
approved a motion to postpone the proceedings indefinitely in part

because of the view, expressed by Lord Grenville, that the power of removal by address was intended to apply only where a judge was either physically incapacitated or where he had been tried and convicted of a crime.

585 Curzon, *English Legal History,* 210.

586 *Comment,* Boston University Law School, Constitutional Processes for the *Discipline of Judges in Massachusetts, 1972 Annual Survey of Mass. Law,* 679, 682-683.

587 Petition of Pittsfield, May 1776, cited in Cella, "The People of Massachusetts, A New Republic and the Constitution of 1780," 930-988.

588 Ibid., 995-96.

589 Dalton, Wirkkala and Thomas, *Leading The Way: A History of the Massachusetts General Court,* 54-56; Edward Hennessey, "The Extraordinary Massachusetts Constitution of 1780," 880-882.

590 Unfortunately, there are no records of the debates of the Constitutional Convention of 1779-1780. A journal does exist, but it provides no information with respect to any discussion or debate around the bill of address.

591 Cella, *Suffolk University Law Review Vol. XIV,* 995.

592 Adams strongly favored good behavior life tenure for judges as a way to ensure their independence. Onello, 1324, n. 20. Adams "was the ideal man to create a compromise constitution for Massachusetts because he held an intermediate position between the radicals and

conservatives, the Berkshire farmers and the Boston merchants." Onello, 1326, n. 28, referring to Nevis.

593 Onello, 1331-1333.

594 *Massachusetts Senate Journal,* March 4, 1803, 339.

595 *Journal of Debates and Proceedings in the Massachusetts Constitutional Convention, 1820-1821,* 482, reprint of original text as published in 1853.

596 Ibid., 629.

597 Ibid.

598 *Commonwealth v. Harriman,* 134 Mass. 314, 316-317 (1883).

JAMES A. ALOISI, JR. has served in several capacities in public service, including as Massachusetts Secretary of Transportation. Between 1996 and 2009, he was a partner in the Boston law firms Hill & Barlow and Goulston & Storrs. He is the author of *The Big Dig,* and *Magic in the Air: The Times & Life of Boston's Honey Fitz.* He divides his time between Boston and Wells, Maine.

green press
INITIATIVE

Ashburton Hill Publishing is committed to preserving ancient forests and natural resources. We elected to print this title on 30% postconsumer recycled paper, processed chlorine-free. As a result, we have saved:

3 Trees (40' tall and 6-8" diameter)
1 Million BTUs of Total Energy
349 Pounds of Greenhouse Gases
1,575 Gallons of Wastewater
99 Pounds of Solid Waste

Ashburton Hill Publishing made this paper choice because our printer, Thomson-Shore, Inc., is a member of Green Press Initiative, a nonprofit program dedicated to supporting authors, publishers, and suppliers in their efforts to reduce their use of fiber obtained from endangered forests.

For more information, visit www.greenpressinitiative.org

Environmental impact estimates were made using the Environmental Defense Paper Calculator. For more information visit: www.edf.org/papercalculator